Conversations with Allende

Conversations with Allende

Socialism in Chile

Régis Debray

VERSO

London • New York

This edition first published by Verso 2023
First published in English by New Left Books 1971
First published as *La via cilena: intervista con Salvador Allende,
presidente del Cile, con una prefazione, e un documento inedito del MIR*
© Giangiacomo Feltrinelli Editore 1971
Translation © Ben Brewster, Peter Beglan,
Marguerita Sanchez, Peter Gowan
Photograph on pages 2 and 3 courtesy of Camera Press
Anniversary edition introduction © Camila Vergara 2023

1 3 5 7 9 10 8 6 4 2

Verso
UK: 6 Meard Street, London W1F 0EG
US: 388 Atlantic Avenue, Brooklyn, NY 11217
versobooks.com

Verso is the imprint of New Left Books

ISBN-13: 978-1-80429-333-1
ISBN-13: 978-1-78873-173-7 (US EBK)
ISBN-13: 978-1-78873-174-4 (UK EBK)

British Library Cataloguing in Publication Data
A catalogue record for this book is available from the British Library

Library of Congress Cataloging-in-Publication Data
A catalog record for this book is available
from the Library of Congress

Printed and bound by CPI Group (UK) Ltd, Croydon, CR0 4YY

Contents

Publishers' note: We wish to express our thanks to Jean Franco for her essential advice in the editing of this English-language edition.

I take this opportunity to thank Claudio Jimeno and Augusto Olivares, whose collaboration made this work possible, and also the Chilean revolutionary leaders and militants who helped me to discover the true features of their country.

R.D.

INTRODUCTION TO THE
ANNIVERSARY EDITION

Introduction to the Anniversary Edition: Legalism and Its Dead Ends by Camila Vergara

The rule of law is not a neutral arrangement of norms and procedures. When law is the result of a political process dominated by elites, in which ordinary people are excluded, only called to the voting booth to authorize a periodic reshuffling of political leadership, the range of possibilities legality can afford to socialism is limited by its elitist constituent element. The attempt by the social-democratic Left to stretch the limits of representative democracy and its bourgeois legality without breaking its rules did not lead to the collapse of old structures and radical transformation, but, rather, to the stabilization of the oligarchic system via 'democratic' credentials. The revisionism that began with Eduard Bernstein at the turn of the twentieth century – opting to make capitalism more egalitarian through state regulation and the fostering of cooperatives with access to cheap credit, rather than radically transforming the production matrix – was revisited, albeit in a different form, with the Cuban Revolution in 1959 and the movements it inspired. With the electoral triumph of Salvador Allende in Chile in 1970, a new possibility opened between the old dichotomy of reform or revolution; Allende's aim was to enact revolutionary reforms to upend the system from within, as Che Guevara's dedication note to Allende in *The Guerrilla War* stated: 'To Salvador Allende, who is trying to obtain the same result by other means.' This crucial moment in revolutionary politics disclosed, on the one hand, the trap of the formalism and proceduralism stemming from the attachment to bourgeois legality as a source of authority and protection against oligarchic domination, and, on the other, the lack of strong popular organizations to defend revolutionary reforms.

The present book is a crucial primary source in the history of revolutionary politics, a snapshot of the first few months after Allende's electoral victory, as seen from the Left. It contains a two-part interview by the French Marxist intellectual Régis Debray with President Allende in early 1971; Debray's introduction to the conversation, providing a materialist account of Chile's political history, an analysis of the 'unstable equilibrium' since Allende had taken office, and a warning against deficient popular organization; and an abridged policy statement by MIR (Movimiento de Izquierda Revolucionaria) released after Allende won the election. Read together, these texts allow for a critical analysis of the electoral strategy chosen by the socialist Left to hack the system from within, through the implementation of radical change using parliamentary institutions. Their analysis of the political context and their prognosis for the 'Chilean road to socialism' via liberal representative democracy allow us not only to better understand revolutionary politics and its challenges in the early 1970s but also to learn from a wisdom moulded in praxis that today seems scarce. Finally, in addition to this collection of intellectual sources, the book is a pedagogical tool, incorporating a useful glossary of popular political history with brief and poignant descriptions of people, parties, and organizations. Overall, the book is an inspiring ride in revolutionary action sprinkled with biographical treasures, analytical tools, and unresolved conundrums.

In his introduction to the conversation with Allende, Debray makes a sharp and prescient analysis of the sociopolitical context in Chile and what was soon likely to unfold. As he insightfully highlights, Chilean political culture is marked by a particular reverence for bourgeois legality and its institutions, based on an 'all-pervading legalism and juridicalism' that has allowed the system to have 'an exceptional capacity for absorption, recuperation and conciliation'. This across-the-board respect for rules and procedures – put in place by elites to remain in power and preserve the status quo – 'has set its seal on the whole social fabric of

Chile', conditioning the conflict between plebeian and oligarchic forces.

While this 'civil' conflict allowed the socialist Left to briefly become government, it also enabled the opposition to dull Allende's blows to the system in Congress while plotting his violent overthrow in the barracks. As Debray notes, this parliamentarian relationship is nefarious for political action from below because it disarms and demobilizes plebeian subjects. 'The Chilean bourgeoisie, one of the least stupid in the world, defends itself by opening its arms to its rival rather than by closing the doors to him . . . draw[ing] him onto its own terrain.' In this way, 'the centre of gravity in the class struggle is transposed and displaced to the level of presidential and parliamentary action in the existing legal political framework – defusing and sublimating the direct action of working-class forces.' Even if the transposition from the politics of streets, assemblies, and unions into that of elections made the victory of the Left possible, for Debray it 'also acts as a brake on its transformation into a complete victory'. The Left is allowed to play the electoral game and even to introduce radical reforms, which are then blunted 'in committee after committee'. The legislative process, monopolized by party elites, is thus a barren land for the seeds of transformation, a terrain that is hostile to radical reforms and that shields elites from 'a frontal attack by popular forces'.

After being elected with a narrow plurality of 36.6 per cent of the vote, and then ratified by a majority in Congress in October 1970, Allende began to swiftly implement the revolutionary reforms contained in the programme of Unidad Popular (UP) – the coalition that brought together the centre-left parties – which entailed the expropriation of foreign-owned mines (accounting for two-thirds of Chilean exports), taking control of almost all national banks and major industrial enterprises, and the expansion of the agrarian reform implemented by the Christian Democrats. Given the radical nature of the programme, counterrevolutionary forces attempted first to prevent Allende's electoral victory, then engaged in covert sabotage and, finally, when all the legal avenues were tried without success, resorted to military force to stop transformation in its tracks. Under President Richard Nixon, the CIA started paying the newspaper of record, *El Mercurio*, to print anti-Allende propaganda in early 1970, and then funded the assassination of René Schneider, the commander-in-chief of the armed forces, who opposed taking action after Allende won the election.* Nixon also imposed an informal economic blockade through American corporations and financial institutions to sabotage the economy, which laid the groundwork for the mobilization of the middle and upper classes in *cacerolazos* (pot bangings) against the government in late 1972. The coup against the UP government was already brewing.

One of Allende's first measures was to nationalize the copper industry through a constitutional amendment that was supported by all parties. The bill declared that the current owners – mainly the US companies Anaconda and Kennecott – would receive compensation, which would be calculated with reference to the 'excessive profits' they had accumulated since 1955. In October 1970, it was declared that the companies owed Chile for their plundering (Kennecott owed US$310 million and Anaconda US$78 million).† In addition, land began to be redistributed at a fast pace with more than 1,300 farms given to the peasantry in the first seven months, and direct public control over industrial production increasing from 10 per cent in 1970 to over 40 per cernt in 1972.‡

* Peter Kornbluh, *The Pinochet File: A Declassified Dossier on Atrocity and Accountability* (New York: New Press, 2003).

† Alan Angell, 'Allende's First Year in Chile', *Current History* 62: 366 (February 1972): 77.

‡ Alan Angell, 'Problems in Allende's Chile', *Current History* 64: 378 (February 1973): 59.

Public spending during Allende's first year in office stimulated economic activity. By 1971, Chile had more than doubled its growth to about 8 per cent, while workers saw real wages increase by 30 per cent, with a 10 per cent shift in national income from capital to labour.[*] However, economic boycott, hoarding, and inflation were already looming, with an increase in consumer prices of 20 per cent in 1971.[†] Within this context, Chile's road to socialism, through revolutionary reforms done within the bounds of the constitution, in which 'the traffic does not seem very dangerous at first sight', made it, for Debray, 'all the more precarious' because the people had not really conquered power but 'merely taken a few forward lines of fortifications in the direction of power'.

In the interview, Debray pushes on two fundamental issues for revolutionary action: the perils involved in relying on legality, both as the terrain of struggle and the source of legitimation and protection, and the primacy given to the revolutionary party and its representatives – despite the denunciation of representative democracy as an elitist game – instead of to popular organizations. Debray calls legality 'the obsessional leitmotif' of the disputes between the government and the opposition in the Chilean national media at that time. He repeatedly questioned Allende about the sustainability of the programme and its protection from counterrevolutionary forces, and the president's response was always the same: one needs to trust the legal authority that is granted when one acts 'by the books', within the bounds of the constitution. Relying on the authority commanded by the triumph of Unidad Popular in the electoral contest, Allende argued that attacks against the government were

[*] Peter Winn, ed., *Victims of the Chilean Miracle: Workers and Neoliberalism in the Pinochet Era, 1973–2002* (Durham: Duke University Press, 2004), 16–17.

[†] Chile Inflation Calculator, World Bank data, 1971–2023 (CLP), *Official Inflation Data*, officialdata.org/chile/inflation.

being pre-empted, 'because this way their hands are tied'. Like a rational model, electoral victory yielded authority to make law, and, if law is established respecting the procedures, it cannot be legally challenged, and therefore it is relatively safe. And if ordinary law was blocked, Allende stated he would resort to a constitutional reform. If that avenue was also foreclosed, he would 'resort to the plebiscite'.

Even if article 109 of the 1925 Constitution empowered the president to call a plebiscite, this provision could only be used if a constitutional reform was rejected by two-thirds of both houses of Congress. Given the structure of parliamentary debate, disagreements were always dealt with in committees and eventually resolved, so a plebiscite was always avoided. This difficult procedure was changed in 1970 under Eduardo Frei to allow the president to call a plebiscite if his proposed constitutional reform 'was totally rejected by Congress, at any stage of the process', making it easier to call on the people to support radical transformation.* Allende's plan was to introduce radical reform by reprogramming the legal mainframe – with the help of the masses, if necessary. Socialism in Chile then was not to be established by decree – Allende was well aware through Lenin of this illusion – but via constitutional reform, backed up by the threat of popular plebiscites.

This movement towards a more plebeian form of constitutional democracy was consistent with the trajectory of the constitution, which was an expression of the political crisis brought about by an elitist parliamentary system that unravelled in the beginning of the twentieth century. As a reaction to elitism, the 1925 juridical order came to engender 'social democracy', a democracy of the masses, in contraposition to the old order in which the elite had political and social

* Guillermo Gandarillas, 'El plebiscito en la Carta de 1925 y en la Reforma de 1970', *Revista de Derecho Público* 13 (1972): 203–5.

supremacy.* By gradually incorporating previously marginalized sectors – women, the poor, and the illiterate – into the political arena and recognizing the social function of property, the 1925 constitution opened the possibility for a radical shift toward popular socioeconomic sovereignty.† This perception enabled four decades of political tensions revolving around the classical conception of property and the need for state intervention in the redistribution of wealth in society. For the most part, this was a *constructive* tension: the ethical debate on the right to property and its redistribution brought about mass-based mobilization and the gradual inclusion of the popular sectors into the power structure, which in turn elevated the quality of life of the lower and middle classes. Allende's aim to use constitutional reform to implement his programme was therefore consistent with this constitutional development and would have allowed the legal order to reach its maximal pro-plebeian potential, initiating a rapid transition from oligarchic democracy to a socialist republic. However, even if it was true that the constitution could be changed 'within the constitution, by means of plebiscites', the same as any procedure and prerogative, plebiscites needed to be used to cease to exist only on paper.

Allende saw the plebiscite as a tool of last resort, but even when it was too late to call one, the plebiscite remained just an idea, a threat of using popular power that never came to fruition. In August 1973, representatives of the Right and the political centre in the Chamber of Deputies accused Allende of twenty violations of the constitution and called upon the military to 'immediately put an end to the situations that infringe

* Julio Heise, *150 años de evolución institucional* (Santiago: Editorial Andrés Bello, 1996), 127. For a complete history of state formation, see Gabriel Salazar and Julio Pinto, *Historia Contemporánea de Chile*, Vols. I–V (Santiago: Lom Ediciones, 1999–2002).

† Renato Cristi and Pablo Ruiz-Tagle, *La República en Chile. Teoría y práctica del Constitucionalismo Republicano* (Santiago: Ediciones LOM, 2006), 116.

the constitution and its laws, and channel governmental actions through the rule of law in order to preserve the constitutional order of our country'.* Even if the agreement was approved in the lower house, the Senate rejected the constitutional removal of the president. To defend himself from these attacks and revalidate his government amid acute crisis, in early September 1973 Allende met with members of his coalition to discuss the possibility of calling a plebiscite on his continuing as president,† but this idea was never turned into a concrete proposal because, according to Minister of Justice Sergio Insunza, the Socialists were against it; they thought that such a plebiscite could not be won.‡ Nevertheless, 'Allende's plebiscite' was openly discussed and used as a threat to oligarchy (calling the plebeian masses onto the political stage, for the first time, to decide on common affairs) and proposed as a solution to the political crisis. Even if Allende never had a concrete plan for a plebiscite, the empty threat hastened military action against him. On 11 September, a CIA-backed military operation bombed La Moneda and took total control of the country, beginning a seventeen-year dictatorship that made of Chile the first laboratory for neoliberal economic policies.§

While legality and respect for procedures did not save Allende and his government, the fragile and incipient nature of the popular organizations meant that what had been already gained could not be protected, and that

* 'Acuerdo de la Cámara de Diputados', *La Nación*, 22 August 1973.

† Such a recall plebiscite was not contemplated in the constitution. The plebiscite could only be on constitutional reform, and therefore Allende would have needed to first introduce an amendment to include a recall vote.

‡ 'Pudimos haber salvado a Allende y a la democracia chilena', *El Mostrador*, 15 September 2003.

§ Arguably, the coup had been in the making for at least a year. On 14 September 1972, Allende had announced the discovery of a 'September Plan' to foment violence as a prelude to a coup. Angell, 'Problems in Allende's Chile', 60.

the people were defenceless against a rising fascist power. According to Debray, plebeian forces had weaknesses related to dislocations of 'class instinct and class consciousness' that led to a 'relative failure of political leadership' and the consequent 'under-mobilization of the mass revolutionary forces'. Even if Allende could definitely mobilize partisans and working-class people to the polls, his focus on the party and on a top-down relation with the masses, instead of prioritizing the establishment of stronger and autonomous popular foundations, contributed to the brittleness of the revolutionary project. When Debray asked him how he proposed 'to transform this electoral mass into a revolutionary mass', Allende responded with a populist-infused Leninism, stating that the 'lines of communication with the people are the parties of the masses in the Popular Unity, which are revolutionary in character', while highlighting his personal and 'direct links with the people'. Much as Nikolay Chernyshevsky's 1860s *narodism* demanded revolutionaries 'go to the people', Allende would often 'meet and talk with squatters, miners, and agricultural workers in the places where they live and work'.

However, the gap between the 'great dedication and great revolutionary fervour' at the top and the 'disorganized and, at times, chaotic' energy that Debray saw in the grassroots could not be easily bridged. Allende's personal closeness to plebeians and the rather weak ties of Left parties and unions to the proletarian and peasant masses were certainly not enough to turn the crowd into a revolutionary subject. Despite popular effervescence and an embryonic organization from below through Popular Unity Committees (CUP), unions, industrial belts (*cordones industrials* – organs of working-class power), and communal assemblies, the government did not attempt to formalize popular spaces of power and, in this way, challenge the foundations of representative oligarchic democracy. Given their organizational precarity, plebeians were neither capable of sustaining an escalating war of movement nor strong enough to maintain one of position that could keep the flame of radical transformation burning under a revitalized 'weight of the night' – the forced compliance that underlies every oligarchic system of rule, no matter how liberal or enlightened.[*]

Perhaps one of the most interesting and underexplored themes in the text, which anticipates Debray's work in 'mediology', was the role played by mass media and the actions that need to be taken to assure the cultural transmission of the socialist society in the making. Allende, following the liberal interpretation of free speech, foreclosed a critical discussion by stating that he would not 'suppress the communications media which are in bourgeois hands, but we are going to coordinate our own'. Even if, under Allende, the public television channel was strengthened and media pluralism was at its highest, with diversity not only of political views but, more importantly, in terms of ownership, conservative oligarchic groups still dominated the media landscape, especially of radio stations, and flooded it with a disinformation campaign that forced the pro-government outlets to engage in barricade-style reporting. This tolerance towards right-wing propaganda rapidly got out of control. By September 1972, *El Mercurio* was openly calling for military intervention and for organizing anti-Marxist paramilitary groups in 'self-defence committees'.[†] Not even the most promising popular media network could have counteracted such a hegemonic narrative subverting the legitimacy of the revolutionary government.

Since the return to democracy in 1990, the media oligopoly has enforced the new neoliberal hegemony

---

[*] This phrase was first used by Diego Portales, the nineteenth-century founder of Chile's authoritarian political culture. For a recent analysis of this notion from the perspective of the 2019 popular uprising, see Rodrigo Karmy Bolton, *El fantasma portaliano* (Santiago: Editorial UFRO, 2022).

[†] 'El quehacer de los medios de comunicación en los años de la Unidad Popular', *Resumen*, 29 August 2020.

that was developed under dictatorial rule. Pinochet's Constitution – drafted by ultraconservative jurists and approved in a fraudulent plebiscite on 11 September 1980 – has been reformed fifty-three times, with 257 of its articles being heavily modified or eliminated. In 2005, after getting rid of the last formal 'authoritarian enclaves', such as the appointed senators for life and the inability to remove the commander of the armed forces, Socialist president Ricardo Lagos declared the transition to a full democracy to be officially concluded and proceeded to sign his name onto the 'new' constitution.* Despite the makeover, the opposition to the Pinochet–Lagos Constitution – which, by then, symbolized a triumphant neoliberal juridical system that had effectively co-opted the parties on the Left – endured.

Fifty years after the military bombed their way into government, and more than three decades into electoral democracy and the deepening of neoliberalism by centre-Left governments, Chile was thrown back into a revolutionary conjuncture. The debate over the redistribution of wealth and political power, which was foreclosed under the dictatorship and then constitutionally negated during thirty years of electoral politics, erupted again with the popular uprising of October 2019. The thousands of local *cabildos* and assemblies, neighbourhood committees, and mutual aid associations that came together during the uprising to demand the end of the Pinochet–Lagos Constitution and the neoliberal order it engendered should be analyzed as part of a long history of a repressed popular democracy that is yet to find its proper constitutional form.

The chaotic popular energy that Debray saw brewing in Chile's plebeian neighbourhoods in 1971 came back in 2019, this time without leaders or party allegiances. Spontaneous mass mobilization and organization at the

---

* For a complete list of these enclaves, see Robert Barros, *La Junta Militar, Pinochet y la Constitución de 1980* (Santiago: Editorial Sudamericana, 2005).

local level, and the relentless resistance to brutal police repression that resulted in hundreds of eye mutilations, were strong enough to force open a constituent process, but not organized enough to direct it. The popular movement and its incipient grassroots organizations were once again frustrated by an imposed electoral process that gave veto power to establishment forces and impeded binding popular participation. Once again, plebiscites were seen as a way both to empower plebeians by granting them decision-making power and to bypass the conservative veto. This time, the plebiscite idea was given concrete form, but it was ultimately rejected even by those claiming to represent the social movements inside the Constitutional Convention. Despite the limitations of the process, the 2022 draft constitution was one of the most progressive constitutions ever written, codifying a broad range of socioeconomic rights and establishing an incipient hybrid constitutional structure in which communal organizations were granted decision-making power – in continuity with Allende's project of radical reform. In the same way as in 1972, the oligarchic media responded to the constituent process and its potential for popular empowerment as an existential threat, spreading disinformation and lies that scared people into rejecting the draft.

This failure to dismantle the neoliberal order within the bounds of the constitution not only emboldened conservative forces, who saw their opposition to radical reform validated at the polls, but also moved the political dial further to the Right. The new president, Gabriel Boric, who won the presidency in coalition with the Communist Party against Pinochet apologist José Antonio Kast, ended up embracing all the conditions imposed by the right-wing parties for a new constituent process that would effectively negate the constituent power and produce a sanitized version of the current neoliberal charter. The new process includes a list of twelve precommitments guaranteeing continuity with the 1980 Constitution, blocking devolution of power and subordinating the realization of rights to 'fiscal responsibility'; a draft constitution written respecting these precommitments by a committee of 'experts' appointed by political parties in which the Right and Christian Democrats have enough seats to veto; a fifty-member Constitutional Council, elected using the same rules as the Senate, where the Right controls half the seats, which will edit the draft under the supervision of an 'admissibility committee'; and finally, as an attempt to legitimize this carefully engineered oligarchic process, a mandatory national plebiscite. This is a nightmarish version of Allende's dream of having a constituent process to radically transform oppressive structures. It forces us not only to reckon that attempting to 'transition from a bourgeois system to another more democratic, more revolutionary, more proletarian system . . . without a break' is likely to be a failure, but also that it could lead to a further entrenchment of the current neoliberal system by stripping it from its less palatable authoritarian legacy and varnishing it with democratic credentials.

Debray's conversation with Allende about strategy and the challenges of revolutionary change without a radical break brings to the fore the contradictions present in the revolutionary process and the specific challenges posed by adhering to legality and the parliamentary process. His insightful analysis, which saw the capacity of conservative forces to condition, co-opt, and neutralize attempts at structural transformation, help illuminate the current counterrevolution and the necessary conditions to resist it.

Popular Chile has aroused a cruel enemy which is now sleeping with one eye open and is ready to spring, to break its institutional trammels, to throw away its ethical inhibitions and to cast off its own restraints. A dangerous enemy because fear makes it aggressive. Can popular Chile face up to it? Can it do so in time?

April 2023

Introduction by Régis Debray

I

Lovers of the epic are asked to spend their holidays elsewhere: 'lyrical illusion' is not current in Chile. In a continent where every lieutenant-colonel gives three speeches a day on the National Revolution, the Chileans have to be satisfied with a government which modestly calls itself 'popular'. The punctilious prose of speeches, of editorials in the major newspapers, of television discussions, of parliamentary debates and of the principal ongoing polemics will thrill no one, unless he is a graduate in Constitutional Law. The principal objects of these disputes are whether this bill is legal, whether that nationalization decree is or is not within the powers of the Executive, whether the workers have not inadvertently misinterpreted some article of the Constitution in throwing out a bankrupt factory owner. From top to bottom of the administrative hierarchy, from one end of the country to the other, the front of the stage is occupied by an interminable legal wrangle, its terms provisions of the legal code, verdicts in the lower courts, grounds for a decision, counter-charges and appeals. The key word in all these disputes, deliberately inflated to the dimensions of a national drama by the bourgeoisie and its means of communication, is not Revolution, or Justice, or Liberation, or Proletariat, but Legality, the tabu term, the obsessional *leitmotif*, and the visible stake. Since jurisprudence is limited in these questions and no one yet knows precisely who is the arbiter or who has the last word – in the Popular Government, in the Supreme Court, in Parliament and perhaps one day among the interested parties themselves – there is enormous confusion and interest is rapidly waning. But then one realizes that this whole spectacle is a *trompe-l'oeil*, and that the reality behind this screen resembles neither a court-room, nor a tribunal, nor a panel discussion, but a closed field in which exploited and exploiters, peasants and big landowners, workers and trusts, patriots and imperialists, directly confront one another in every corner of the country.

A subtle and dangerous game is being played in Chile – its seriousness less and less disguised by the appearance of cordial urbanity which is supposed to be the hall-mark of the Chilean. Up to now, at least, despite a few snags, it really has been a 'game'. Each of the two camps observes pre-ordained rules (established by one of the partners and to his advantage), respected willy-nilly by both sides: the rules of the free play of the 'democratic institutions' in force in a liberal republic. Although it has been proved that the game is not entirely above board in the bourgeois camp, at any rate the game is still being played. Foul blows are allowed, but not officially counted in the score; a blind eye is turned to them. For how long? 'Formal bourgeois democracy might just last three months more', said a revolutionary leader, himself a Senator of the Republic, a little while ago, 'Then comes the crunch.' This prognosis is disputable, the postponement could be extended. But what is certain is that the path from polite hatred to open hostilities is shorter than either side had thought; today there is a bizarre state of truce, tense and brittle, which is not really peace without yet being war, and which may be broken any day. The course of events accelerates as the class antagonisms get more acute, without it yet being possible to predict the concrete form and the moment of their resolution. Everything confirms that this is a contradictory process whose solution and result will not be met with inside the conditions in which it has developed up till now. The crisis of definition has not yet exploded. Even at the most superficial political level there has been no revolutionary 'break'. At first sight it seems impossible to register a 'before' and an 'after' anywhere: in the uniform of the carabinieri, in the faces of passers-by, in the names of public buildings, or in the Saturday motor-car rush to the sea-side – nowhere is there a suggestion that a new world might be born here. And yet, from previously given conditions, difficult to handle but impossible to elude, a complex gestation has begun which no one can be certain at this stage will not end by giving birth to a really new society freed from exploitation and foreign domination. However subtle the transition, Chile is committed to an irreversible historical experiment, such that if it fails to reach its goal, it is hard to see how it could return to its starting-point. This country is no longer far from the threshold of that dangerous zone in which the people are condemned to win or lose all (at least for the time being), in which no half-measures, no sleight of hand can save them from the historical alternative: Revolution or Counter-Revolution.

The real stake: first, of course, the future of the Chilean nation and people, the emancipation of its workers, their achievement of humane living conditions. That the Chilean people constitute themselves as the protagonists of their own history – that is the aim, and it is also the pre-condition for reaching that aim: the apparently vicious circle on which everything depends. From today, they must begin to take their future into their own hands, if they do not want their enemies to steal it from them tomorrow by brute force, or to sneak it away as usual – e.g. by an electoral conjuring-trick in a few years' time. The date of expiry seems a long way off – the popular government has just been elected and, according to the Constitution, it remains in power for six years; in fact, everything suggests that time is short.

But at this particular moment, the stake is also the future of the surrounding countries – through the dia-lectical bonds which, willy-nilly, objectively link the Latin-American nations to one another; a new rung attained in the progressive inversion of the relations of forces at the continental level, and by the same token, a new stage reached in the burial of imperialism by all the peoples of the world; it is the breakdown of the twelve-year blockade with which the US empire hoped to suffocate Cuba, and first of all to isolate it from the Latin-American continent; it is a new historical experience with consider-able powers of incitement, since it is a trial run for the construction of socialism in a society which, through its very special conditions, has effectively avoided political under-development; it is also – a subordinate, but by no means negligible advantage – a refuge for exiled or persecuted revolutionaries. Even if the Chileans do not realize it, what happens – or does not happen – in Chile concerns first and foremost the whole of Latin America. The results of this dangerous game, whether negative or positive, will mark a stage in the international class struggle, a turning-point for the armed continental Revolution. On the fate ultimately accorded this 'revolution without rifles', as it has been provisionally – and somewhat optimistically – called, depends the fate of many other rifles.

This result in turn largely depends on the political leadership the popular movement has acquired. It depends on its imagination and on its realism, on its prudence and on its daring, on its patriotism and on its internationalism, i.e. on the way it combines the first with the second, fusing them into a correct political practice. This leadership has fallen to a united front of various parties. But it can be found in concentrated form in the astonishing and extremely effective mixture of calmness and resolution, of tactical flexibility and strategic firmness, united in the personality of the '*Compañero Presidente*', Salvador Allende. Hence the truly political interest of the disjointed conversation you are about to read.

The foreign traveller, French in this case, who has managed to keep a few oddments of historical materialism in his memory, and who by an unexpected chance is deposited one day in the North of Chile with a fortnight's tourist visa, is exposed to more than one disappointment if he perseveres in trying to grasp an ungraspable situation. Translated immediately into canonic terms – into 'basic Marxist-Leninism' – it becomes incomprehensible, irritating, even disturbing. The endless train of perplexities destroys one's bearings. To begin at the beginning: when last for example, did a bourgeoisie hand its power to its class enemy on a silver platter? When last did a ruling class allow itself to be shown to the door of history without risking everything to stay put? Seen from outside and

at a distance, this is how the Popular Unity seems to have
come to power, respecting at each stage the protocol
of presidential permutations at the apex of the existing
system. In fact, this theoretical scandal is very quickly
cleared up once one finds on the spot that the question
posed was quite simply without an object. That is, in the
first place, that the bourgeoisie in power – the governmental apparatus, military reaction, the great national
and foreign monopolist interests, their political representatives – tried everything, possible and impossible, to bar
the road to the Presidency to Salvador Allende and the
Popular Unity: an odious and grotesque story which
will one day doubtless be completely uncovered by the
right people, and in which the assassination of the Army
Commander-in-Chief only constitutes one episode. And, in
the second place, that the popular forces have not conquered power, they have merely taken a few forward lines
of fortifications in the direction of power. In this sense,
the theoretician's apprentice, better informed, no longer
needs to be shocked; for all that, his tranquillity will not
come back to him, but for different reasons, as we shall
see.

Nevertheless, it remains the case that the popular forces,
such as they are in Chile, entered the government legally
and without firing a shot. Before asking what they aim to
do with this situation in the future, one can ask how, at
this moment, they have been able to get to this point.
This very special conjuncture – the period of the elections
and of the *'transmision del Mando'* – must be grasped
at its true level, at the level of a very precise political
struggle, susceptible to a finer analysis in which fractions
of classes and intermediate strata should be discussed
rather than two antagonistic camps. Nevertheless, it is
essential to go beyond competitions between different
political formations and the personal rivalries of leaders
in order to understand how the play of logical class re-
groupments and fundamental solidarities of interest could
turn up the wrong card in the electoral period. The
Chilean bourgeoisie was unable to forge a Holy Alliance

in time when confronted with the rise of conscious popular forces, because it does not constitute an abstract entity, a bloc of globally compatible interests, susceptible to reflection as such at the level of the struggle for political power. In 1964, the Chilean ruling class had allowed itself to be represented in power by its Christian Democrat fraction, and by it alone, against the representative of the conscious socialist forces. In 1970, against the same representative, it was no longer capable of re-forming this unity, either ideologically or politically. What had happened in between?

Delegated to its post by the bourgeoisie, Christian Democracy in power for six years built up the conditions for a revolutionary process, against its will, of course: it cleared the ground by its verbal populism for real popular conquests; it underlined and legitimized the need to take radical measures by its clumsy velleities; it raised the threshold of ideological tolerance in the middle strata, the core of its clientele. Even if in fact the Agrarian Reform, after an initial timid application, turned into a simple transaction with the old agrarian bourgeoisie; even if the 'Chileanization' of the country's basic wealth, the copper mines, turned in practice into a pact negotiated according to the interests and to the advantage of the North American trusts – there remained the grand slogans of agitation and propaganda brandished at every level, with the petulance of a sorcerer's apprentice, by a petty-bourgeois leadership, modernist but wary, moralizing but too cunning to be honest. The contradictions of this dependent capitalist society were so deep and insoluble that, to protect the basic interests of the ruling class, the most enlightened fraction of the bourgeoisie was forced to risk these interests in a gamble which it finally lost. Christian Democracy was the first victim of its own instrument of ideological rule. In fact, inside its reformist project – the integration of the unorganized subordinate classes into the reigning system of exploitation in order to modernize its mechanisms and ensure a higher profitability – there developed at the base a spontaneous mass movement of a revolutionary kind, which inevitably overflowed the bounds set by the project itself. For example, by legalizing and instigating unions of poor peasants and agricultural workers in the country (counter-balanced, it is true, by the parallel formation of '*gremios*' of the large landowners), and by authorizing embryonic forms of communal organization in the urban sectors, it accelerated the development of class consciousness among the exploited, workers and unemployed, and raised the level of their social aspirations, without, however, being able to satisfy these aspirations. 'Social Christianity' constructed generous plans of 'popular promotion', but the people quickly went beyond the promoters, even to the extent of demanding an explanation from them, thus demonstrating the truth that it is impossible to bring into question the authoritarian and vertical forms of bourgeois rule without ultimately bringing into question the economic foundations of that rule, i.e. the exploitation of labour power itself, the private ownership of the means of production and finally the whole system of a profit economy. It is a dangerous utopia to offer the masses participation in political power without being prepared to see hands laid on the bases of one's own economic power. In this way, the predecessors of the popular government unwittingly released a movement which threatened to submerge them and which eventually terrified many of them. In the last years of the petty-bourgeois government, the repressive nucleus hidden in every reformist project, the anti-popular core concealed by every populist project, had already come into the open. Unable in social practice to perform the tasks it proposes for itself in its political programme, a reformist undertaking sooner or later splits to give place on the one hand to those who are prepared to take the political undertaking to its conclusions regardless of its social consequences, i.e. without retreating from the class struggle, and on the other, to those who throw overboard the political programme to protect their class interests. The former are *en route* for proletarian class positions, the latter remove their masks, revealing once and for all their true class nature. When the social being of a political group comes into contradiction with its social consciousness, when economic interests clash with spiritual interests, a period of internal crisis begins, and this is what shook and fractured Christian-Democracy in its decline, thus revealing its nature as a heterogeneous conglomerate spanning the divide between the camps. Indeed, in its own way, more refined and mediated than elsewhere, but also more obvious because of its privileged political development, Chile experienced the imperious law according to which it is impossible in Latin America today to initiate a bourgeois-democratic revolution without rapidly unleashing a process of socialist revolution; it is impossible to avoid the second while waving the flag of the first.

In 1970, at the moment of elections which were to offer government to the socialist left, a locomotive was on the rails, it had gathered speed and threatened very shortly to break through all the established barriers. Faced with this phenomenon, the ruling class and its political general staffs split in two: the partisans of a rapid return to the hierarchic and authoritarian system of traditional rule, terrified by the process initiated six years earlier, decided at all costs to apply the basic brake – the Legitimate Right, represented by Alessandri. But those who wished to remain at the controls of the machine (either to restrain it and prevent it from going too far, or quite simply because they did not mind the speed) – Christian Democracy, illegitimate grand-daughter of the Ancestral Right (by the Phalange and the Conservative Party), bastard offspring ogling the left with one eye, united in support of Radomiro Tomic, its openly 'leftist' candidate, extremist of Christian morality. Tomic chose the right as his main enemy, thus becoming an objective and personal ally of the Popular Unity candidate, behind the back and even against the will of his own governmental apparatus. An aberration which still makes the bourgeoisie grind their teeth, and which its official representative, the former President Frei, who publicly laments it, will be slow to forgive. An aberration which ceases to be an aberration once one remembers that an ideology (like the 'communitarian and personalist' one promulgated by Christian Democracy) is not just a propaganda ruse, an instrument of deceit cynically manipulated from outside which can be abandoned once the tool no longer serves its purpose; once one remembers that an organized form of social consciousness, however imaginary, englobes its adherents as their own world, spontaneously lived as the real world. It can be that the propagandist is convinced in good faith, for the bearers of ideology are also its objects, and sometimes its victims.

The present situation in Chile is no disproof of the principles of Marxist interpretation – it merely disproves dogmatic distortions of the latter. The universal principles of Marxism-Leninism still have to be applied to this concrete reality in everyday action, and this task is the exclusive responsibility of the Chilean vanguards. But a historical rationality has also still to be found for this unique conjuncture, for the present political struggle – and this is a collective task of analysis in which anyone, whoever he is, can put forward a hypothesis. To account in fact for the 'current moment', the product of a complex past, it is necessary to turn to a history of Chile since its independence, at any rate to the outline of such a history.

II

We should not be surprised that, today as yesterday, Chile has set out to explore the possibilities of the epoch as a scout, somewhat ahead of its neighbours. Every historian of Latin America knows that this laboratory for social experiment anticipated the development of the Continent by producing the first workers' friendly societies ('Sociedad de artesanos', in 1847, without the slightest trace of class consciousness, of course), the first railway (1852), the most advanced civil legislation for its time (Andres Bello, 1855), the first social legislation actually put into practice (the law of Sunday rest, 1907, simultaneously with Batlle's Uruguay), one of the best education

systems, lay and compulsory (1909), the first Socialist
Republic in America (1932, so baptized by order-in-
council after Marmaduke Grove's *coup d'état*), the first,
if not the only Popular Front in the Continent (1938),
etc. . . . Elsewhere in this part of the world, it would be
hard to find such a precociously constituted bourgeoisie,
so sure of itself and expansionist, just as it would be hard
to find a workers' movement so firmly installed on its class
positions since the beginning of the century. It is as if
emerging liberalism and emerging socialism, bourgeois
forms of development and socialist forms of development,
had together and in competition chosen this dependent
capitalist country for their first hazardous Latin-American
appearances, for their first footholds on the Continent.

Hence it is no accident that the first Latin-American
nation, after Cuba, which has found itself on a road
to socialism, its own road to socialism, should be this
particular one. And yet it would be simplistic to conclude
from what can be seen happening here that the imperialist
chain is beginning to break (or might break in the near
future) at its weakest link. Lenin's metaphor must be
handled with care, for precisely by virtue of the flexibility
and old foundations enjoyed by the forms of bourgeois
political rule in Chile, this country may appear on the
contrary as the link in the continental chain the most
likely to resist the strongest popular pressure, as the most
flexible and not the weakest, the most elastic and *for that
very reason the most resistant* link. And if the chain of
regimes of exploitation has suffered a sharp blow at this
point in the Continent and not elsewhere, this may be
because the link most likely to stretch without breaking lies
at this very point. This paradox has not escaped the State
Department which formulated it in its own vocabulary
after Allende's victory out of the mouths of those 'well-
informed observers' sponsored by the US propaganda
agencies (Associated Press or United Press) in their
Washington-inspired cables: 'After all, we should not get
too worked up about "the Marxist Allende", for this is
not the first time we have had Communist ministers in the

government. Chile has had them before, in 1938 and 1946, and yet it did not leave the democratic fold.' But after the popular victory in Chile, this same State Department also sent instructions to all the US diplomatic missions in Latin America, ordering them to harden their attitude and not to permit themselves the slightest tolerance towards liberal tendencies: Chile has become the main enemy of the moment. For imperialism, this is the time for firmness, the gorillas must be made aware that their patron is behind them. And never have so many tourists, advisers and counsellors with diplomatic passports, journalists and investigators of every kind descended on Santiago in such a short time before. In other words, the enemy has found some reassuring and some disturbing arguments. The same arguments the other way round urge revolutionaries to be vigilant and keep a cool head – nothing has yet been won – while looking confidently into the future – nothing has been lost in advance: given the objective conditions, everything depends on the quality of the choices made. The enemy, who is not certain which saint to turn to or on what leg to stand, is on the alert, hostile but still reserved. The Chilean revolutionaries, the conscious working class, base and vanguard of the anti-imperialist struggle, can turn this precious delay to their advantage by grasping and keeping the initiative.

Anyone prepared to accept a cavalier view of the Chilean past – the genesis and formation of contemporary Chile – anyone who can afford an elevated perspective (the privilege of passing observers who for lack of time examine the historical map of the country they are flying over from an aeroplane window) will see this geographically crazy but historically reasonable strip of land stand out clearly enough against the Latin-American background, since institutions of formal democracy and advanced forms of the workers' movement have each seen an equally extensive development there. In Chile, proletariat and bourgeoisie have *together* reached a level of consciousness and organization higher than elsewhere. The distinctive feature, the originality of Chilean history, the general tone, perhaps, the atmosphere which gives its peculiar colouring to this long and bitter class struggle, can be found in the combination of these two simultaneously solidary and antagonistic elements. Only Uruguay used once to offer a similar picture in a much attenuated form, but today this has been almost completely effaced by the dynamic of the revolutionary struggle and the decomposition of the liberal State there. And to restrict myself to a neighbouring country in which I had occasion to spend some time, if in Bolivia there exists a marked contrast between the two arms of the class scales, it is one in which, from a qualitative point of view, a super-proletariat is counter-posed to a sub-bourgeoisie of such little weight that it must constantly re-establish the balance with repressive force of arms, or even make way for that modern *ersatz* bourgeoisie, a military bureaucracy torn between vertiginous reformist velleities and its reflex reactionary fear of the rise of workers' power.

Not that Chilean history really is like the suave democratic idyll with which it is often confused. It is certainly, but in a rather underground way, one of the most violent and perhaps the most bloody histories in Latin America, both in the last century's civil wars between patriots and royalists, conservatives and liberals, clericals and anticlericals, nationalists and pro-imperialists (the often distorted reflections of divergent class interests within the ruling class), and from the beginning of this century, in the frequency of great murderous manoeuvres by the repressive apparatus against the workers and peasants, culminating in ferocious episodes. So we still need to explain how the image of a peaceful and liberal Chile gained currency even inside the country and is accepted as indisputable by the vast majority – bourgeois coercion transposed to the level of persuasive mythology. We still have to explain how the sporadic and endemic violence of the class confrontations never seriously upset the stability of representative institutions, or rather, how Chile succeeded in sparing itself the interminable military dictatorships which were and remain the rule elsewhere, while remaining for all that a country subjected by a voracious oligarchy.

Over and above its momentary upsets – there have been some, but they were short-lived – liberal bourgeois democracy, which has set its seal on the whole social fabric of Chile until today, has demonstrated an exceptional capacity for absorption, recuperation and conciliation. It has provided and continues to provide a ruling ideology, the still all-pervading legalism and juridicalism; open-armed political structures, the stable institutional framework; and a whole system of representations lived at the humblest level, the myths of Liberty and Law with capital Ls which penetrate even the attitudes of the exploited. It will not disappear in the blink of an eye, not even if the present State were overthrown tomorrow; the whole of 'civil society' is steeped in it. In this sense Chile belongs to those 'Western' societies discussed by Gramsci, in which the main fortress of the State, always vulnerable to a lucky stroke, is backed up rank on rank by a whole network of trenches, strong points and bastions whose conquest 'is not so simple. To explain this objective fact by tradition, national character, the racial peculiarities of the Araucanians or the spirit of Diego Portales is merely to push the problem back a stage: one might as well attribute the action of sleep to its dormitive virtue or feelings of inferiority to an inferiority complex. Scholastic or mystical, these tautologies get us nowhere. Is the explanation then that the predominance of the 'democratic' idea and of 'democratic' rules in Chile corresponds to a privileged economic development? Not at all: all the current economic indices, all statistical references place Chile among the so-called under-developed countries (i.e. among the capitalist countries subordinate to the world imperialist metropoles), ahead of Guatemala or Paraguay, but behind Venezuela or Mexico. The loss of the great nitrate and copper mines to foreign control at the end of the last century, the inability to incorporate the gains of an industrial revolution, restricted to enclaves producing raw materials for export, into the framework of a national economy, the increasing technological backwardness of the productive apparatus under the influence of foreign monopolies, have produced a relative stagnation of the contemporary capitalist production system, whose rise was cut off half-way. This dissociation between an economic base today relatively behind those of its great neighbours and an advanced political organization constitutes precisely the heart of the problem, Chile's strangeness. In fact, to explain it we must look backwards, towards the historical formation of the Chilean nation. A whole range of factors help to explain the constitution and maintenance of this superstructural constant with its relative autonomy and durability.

I shall attempt to list the main ones, from the simplest to the most complex: the notable conflicts of influence throughout the nineteenth century between British and North-American imperialism, joined by Germany towards the end of the century, neutralizing one another to some extent; the country's geographical remoteness from the centres of world power; a precocious economic growth immediately after the proclamation of independence, in contrast with the long depression which was the fate of the young Latin-American republics after the Wars of Independence, and is reflected in baroque caudillism, generalized anarchy and finally in the inability of these landed oligarchies to found anything like a national state. Chile, on the contrary, experienced a relatively harmonious transition without serious shocks, from a mercantilist colonial economy, primarily exporting agricultural goods (grain, leather), to a primarily extractive economy (the basic wealth passing from silver mines at the beginning of the last century to coal, iron and copper mines and then to the nitrate deposits in the North, with finally, after the First World War, a return in force to the exploitation of the copper mines), a base on which, at the beginning of the twentieth century, it was in turn possible to build and even initially to finance autonomously a productive apparatus of light and transformatory industries. The elasticity of this economic structure and the steadiness of its expansion thus favoured political compromises between ruling classes and class fractions, by a series of amalgamations and absorptions, through a slow assimilation of the respective interests of latifundists, mine-owners, financiers and industrialists. The more than century-old economic pedigree of the Edwards clan, symbol and spearhead of the Chilean oligarchy, provides a typical example of these capital transfers, of this network of ramifications and alliances stretching from mines to big land-holdings, from the land to usury, then from banks to industry and finally to the control of political power and of the means of communication (the Edwards family owns the *Mercurio*, the biggest and most 'prestigious' Chilean newspaper, a national institution in bourgeois eyes and a mortal enemy of the popular government). Despite the friction and the clashes, the momentary fractures in these alliances, despite the spasmodic civil wars throughout the nineteenth century between Conservatives and Liberals, notably over the religious question, despite the oligarchic 'Revolution' which drove President Balmaceda to suicide in 1891 and in which a recently formed industrial bourgeoisie was forced to abdicate in favour of a more solidly based agrarian and commercial oligarchy – in general, mutual concessions have ultimately prevailed over internal dissensions. After 1895, the latter tended to move into the background with the emergence of a threatening workers' movement. Moreover, we should stress here the national specificity of big landed property – the historical base of the oligarchic pyramid – which is quite unlike the agrarian structures of the Central American republics, for example, or that of Mexico before the Revolution. In Chile there have never been massive foreign investments in the agricultural sector (except for a few unimportant present-day enclaves at Magallanes in the South), and bourgeois governments, including Frei's, have always demonstrated a marked resistance to North-American offers to buy land. Foreign penetration is confined to the new agricultural-industrial sector (technical equipment, commercial distribution networks, etc.). Thus, this national agrarian infrastructure provided the basis for an *haute bourgeoisie* of industrialists and bankers who did not despise the internal market, and were endowed with considerable national autonomy, at the beginning at least: e.g. the first banks which appeared in Chile in the 1860s all had Chilean names. Modern capitalism did not arrive in Chile as foreign capitalism in the train of an invader or as the price of political independence; it was steadily penetrated by and alienated to British imperialism and then to North America in a further and relatively late stage of its development. If we add to these various factors the rapid construction of a powerful military machine – a Land Army and Navy – technically in advance of those of neighbouring countries, the victory over Peru and Bolivia in the War of the Pacific (1879), the resultant territorial annexations and economic expansion, it is clearer why the Chilean ruling class was able at its formation to constitute itself as a 'national class' capable of presenting its particular interests as the interests of the nation as a whole, even in the eyes of the subordinate classes, why it has been able to give its forms of political rule a long undisputed moral legitimacy, strength and arrogance.

It is also clear why, almost alone among its fellows at the time, the Chilean oligarchy in the last century was able to constitute a centralized State apparatus and to develop in all its forms the legal-political ideology adapted to the correct functioning of that apparatus. The treasury's revenues, derived from foreign trade, quickly made it possible to maintain a State bureaucracy, a whole complex and relatively well organized stratum of officials. The tradition of State service and the public function of political training had no equal in Latin America until very recently. Even the Army was transformed by it into a bureaucratic corps, subject to the central civil authority and to the ruling legal-political ideology, a mere instrument and not the source of bourgeois rule, its auxiliary not its palliative, and therefore unlikely to stand in for the bourgeoisie for long in the exercize of political power, for the simple reason that the bourgeoisie had no need of the

Army for that purpose: as a whole, the bourgeoisie showed that it was capable of playing its part directly, i.e. of performing its historical tasks as collector of the economic surplus and architect of the national State. It had no need of a military substitute for long periods. In the 1930s, this pre-existing politico-administrative structure had also to permit and encourage the birth of the first organs of a State capitalism, and later, with the rise to power of Christian Democracy, the appearance of a plan for the technocratic regulation of social conflicts from above, a plan whose effects are still felt today.

It was possible to set up such a State apparatus, with its routine, its internal control mechanisms (e.g. the 'Controlaria General de la República', created in 1927), its training schools, its comparatively elevated ethical norms, largely because the oligarchy did not need it for a living, because the control or usufruct of this politico-administrative apparatus did not represent one of its means of subsistence. Hierarchic relations being inscribed in the 'nature of things' (in the last instance, in the relations of production), individual enrichment having been achieved previously in private economic activity, personal or familial success was naturally crowned and consecrated by a political career (senator, minister, president, ambassador or even, as a beginning, head of department), but it was not obtained by way of it. Hence the respectability and seriousness of what is called 'politics' in Chile – a socially recognized activity which the best society can, and even must, take part in without demeaning itself, governed by certain rules of *savoir-vivre* and mutual respect: in general, an association of rival 'clubmen' and not, as is traditional in most of the bourgeois dictatorships of the Continent, which are not all comic-opera dictatorships by any means, a mortal knife-fight, a public Mafia, a rubbish heap or employment agency for lucky black sheep. Hence another striking feature of oligarchic Chile, hardly in conformity with the surrounding environment: ministers, presidents and generals have not systematically enriched themselves by the exercise of their functions.

Corruption can be said to have been the exception and not the rule, and that is exceptional. Hence that genuine familiarity and patrician distinction which, till a little while ago, meant that 'decent people' did not exterminate one another, even if they were in opposite camps – at most exile or a few weeks in prison for the most recalcitrant opponent. The last political assassination before that of the Army Commander-in-Chief in 1970 was the murder of Portales, the author of the 1833 Constitution, in 1837. Until the Alessandri epoch, a few years ago – which shows how time flies – it was possible to bump into the President of the Republic in the street, returning on foot to his apartment in the Moneda Palace, just like any other citizen. A banal anecdote, but one symptomatic of a now abolished equilibrium.

Such is the first element of an historical analysis, the simplest element to bring to light, the most presentable side of the coin: the classical character, measured by European norms (or aberrant, if you prefer, measured by norms held to be typically Latin-American), that bourgeois hegemony has taken in Chile. Comparison with England or France – and it is true that English political economy and French political thought have played their part in the formation of Chile – is a ritual and ideological cliché which is not unflattering to the local oligarchy and at any rate does not seem to insult its national pride. Besides, remembering that the 1833 Constitution remained in force for almost a century (the nationalist president Balmaceda was driven from office at the end of the last century in the name of respect for the established Constitution), and that the 1925 Constitution, fundamentally in line with the precepts of the previous one, still regulates the minutiae of everyday life in the country today, we can see straightaway that European liberal democracies, France for example, with its changing regimes and revolving republics, look like banana republics in comparison with Chile. And yet, this element alone will not explain Chile's idiosyncracy. It only constitutes one pole of a dialectical relationship, and it is this relationship which is original in Latin America, not each of its terms by themselves.

This hegemonic framework was already in position when, at the end of the last century, a vigorous but still chaotic movement of working-class protest appeared, followed by spontaneous mass rebellions and growing in the twenties into a real workers' movement, organized on independent class positions. The urban population, 38 per cent of the total in 1895, rose to 43 per cent by 1907; i.e. even before the end of the last century, an already initiated industrialization process had made a growing number of peons (*inquilinos*), agricultural labourers and poor peasants move into the mining centres and nitrate camps on the outskirts of the towns. At the beginning of this century, under the influence of an élite of artisans and skilled workers, sometimes of foreign extraction and anarchist or anarcho-syndicalist in persuasion, this new working class, formerly grouped into apolitical friendly societies, was organized into *mancomunales*, or unions of combative resistance. The proletariat's struggle against the inhuman living conditions provided for it by foreign companies, particularly in the labour camps of *la pampa salitrera*, beginning in the 1880s, took on violent forms. It was a struggle for survival and the ruling class it confronted proved a ruthless one. The Army intervened more than once, and shot to kill. The list of bloody strikes and *matanzas*, massacres, punctuating the struggle of the Chilean proletariat and peasantry, is endless: from the first great strike of port-workers in Valparaiso in 1903 (30 dead, 200 wounded), the 'meat strike' in Santiago in 1905 (200 killed), the massacre of Santo-Maria at Iquique, the cradle of the workers' movement, in 1907 (more than 2,000 victims, mown down by machine-gun in the city square), the Punta Arenas massacre of 1920, the Coruña massacre of 1925 (3,000 killed in the saltpetre mines), the massacre of peasants at Ranquil in 1934 (60 dead), to the recent exploits of Christian Democracy at the El Salvador mine in 1966, via the Santiago riots of April 1957; all signs of an impulsive, pre-civilized class struggle underlying the history of political struggles strictly speaking, but ruthless and of a cruelty hard to fit into the picture-postcard image of a debonair and affectionate Chile. The rules of the civilized game do not apply to the exploited, the marginal, the disenfranchized, but then the latter do not write the official history. Nevertheless, this sporadic violence would only have a limited significance if it did not relate to a truly political event, and a very far-reaching and exceptional one: *the union of Marxist theory and the national workers' movement*. This union crystallized after the Soviet Revolution with the foundation of the Chilean Workers' Federation (FOCH), affiliated to the Red Trade Union International (Concepción Congress, 1919), and with the transformation of the Socialist Workers' Party into the Communist Party in 1921, under the influence and aegis of Recabarren, once a printing worker and anarchist. Of course, Communist Parties and revolutionary organizations were founded sooner or later in almost every Latin-American country. But in Chile they emerged from within the workers' movement and drew their life-blood from the class itself, from its everyday economic and social struggles, plunging their roots into its depths. The product of this union had its ups and downs, and only a minority of conscious workers was able to hold unswervingly to class positions, but it remains the case that Chile is the only country on the Continent (other than Bolivia, but in different forms and earlier) in which the parties called working-class because of their ideologies were also organically working-class in their recruitment and social base. The only country in which the ruling class has had to face a century's defiance from a proletarian resistance movement which it has not succeeded in reducing in the long run even if it has momentarily managed to isolate or divide it. Whatever the splits, refluxes and rivalries in the history of this workers' movement, it is a fact that it has never ceased to exist directly, drawing its sustenance from proletarian struggles themselves, and not by ideological delegation via intellectual or petty-bourgeois vanguards. To give some idea of its political volume, let me point out that in the parliamentary elections of 1941, the two explicitly Marxist parties, the Communists and the Socialists, obtained 32 per cent of the vote, one third of the electorate, which excludes the illiterate. Nevertheless, the Communist Party was outlawed for long periods (1925–35 and 1948–58, under Alessandri and then under Ibañez), and independent unionism breached more than once; but even in phases of clandestinity or persecution, the workers' organizations managed to survive, to hold and even to gain ground, through the Socialist Party which was still legal, for example, or with the help of the liberal petty-bourgeoisie (whose political parties united in the mass movement for the repeal in 1958 of the 'Accursed Law', styled the Law for the Defence of Democracy, the imported McCarthyite product which banned the Communist Party).

In short, never, even in moments of the greatest national or international tension, did this most reactionary monopolistic bourgeoisie succeed in lastingly 'breaking' the proletarian movement. On the other hand, neither has the latter managed to 'break' or even, until today, seriously to threaten political and economic class rule. The hegemonic framework has held, despite the bitterness of the confrontations and the insistence of working-class pressure. It is clear that realignments and reversals have occurred, sometimes very rapidly, in class relations and alliances, in correspondence with changes in the economic equilibrium, but within the space provided by this framework. For example, what is called the 'crisis of the oligarchy' after 1920, with the rise to power of Arturo Alessandri, can be interpreted as a strategic withdrawal by the landed oligarchy onto defensive, retreating positions, and its relief by a fresh wave, the commercial, financial and industrial bourgeoisie. In the same way, the bourgeoisie later on had to surmount the depressive effects of the world crisis of 1929 by finding room at its side for the urban middle strata (strata without control over the major means of production) and their political expression, radicalism, which moved into the leading role in the new coalition.

These crises correspond to mutations rather than ruptures, shifts in the centre of gravity within the apparatus itself. Or again: not only was the institutional game of liberal democracy kept intact (except for the period 1924–1925, and the period called the period of Anarchy, 1931–1932, which had no lasting repercussions), but the workers' movement, in and beyond the tensions and crises, was transformed into one of the poles necessary for the maintenance, i.e. the periodic re-equilibration, of the system of rule. The Chilean bourgeoisie, one of the least stupid in the world, defends itself by opening its arms to its rival rather than by closing the doors to him. It prefers to admit its opponent's existence in order the better to follow his movements, to draw him onto its own terrain rather than to force him into his last redoubts. To explain how class hostility at the level of social life was ultimately translated and refined into this tense coexistence within a bourgeois-democratic regime at the political level, without lapsing into subjectivist anathemata thrown at the traditional political leaderships, it is again necessary to take into account a certain number of historically determined objective conditions. Firstly, the productive working class has always been scattered or compartmentalized in peripheral mining centres, far from the capital, the centre of political power, in the North (Iquique, Antofagasta, Calama, etc.) or the distant South (Concepción, Lota, Magallanes), so that it was practically impossible to coordinate limited or even insurrectionary struggles divided among centres so remote from one another. The manoeuvrable mass which this proletarian vanguard might have been able to constitute was dislocated from the outset: when the echo of the protest marches, strikes and massacres reached the capital, it had been muffled by the distance. Secondly, the workers' movement, despite the efforts of Recabarren and his successors, failed until very recently to make an organic alliance with the agricultural proletariat and the poor peasantry, and never managed to influence these classes seriously, except on the outskirts of working-class concentrations. The peasantry, isolated in the *fundos*, directly dependent on their boss, often illiterate and in the grip of the clergy, remained the passive clientele of the latifundist oligarchy until ten years ago, and the ruling class had always jealously protected the peasants from any trace of baleful urban influence: until 1937, peasant unionization was illegal and severely repressed, and in 1965 there were still officially only twenty peasant unions with a total of 2,000 members throughout the country. Thirdly, the fact that the organized working class (union and political) was in a minority with respect to the real class – a characteristic reinforced by legislation prohibiting trade-union rights – favoured the electoral capture in periods of retreat of a large number of marginal workers with a still amorphous class consciousness by the bourgeois leaderships (by Alessandri's centrism in the 1920s, or by the younger Ibañez's authoritarian populism *à la Perón* in the 1950s). Finally, the rise of the working class occurred simultaneously with that of the salaried middle classes, starting in 1930, so that the class alliance implied by the strategy of the Popular Front, inevitable anyway, mingled and diluted proletarian interests with those of the petty bourgeoisie, usually to the advantage of the latter. Such are the main factors of a historical kind thanks to which the hegemonic framework has been able to absorb the impact and destructive force of such a powerful workers' movement. Many observers from other Latin-American countries are surprised, when they arrive in Chile, by the level of politicization of the Chilean working class, and of the Chilean people as a whole. The fact is real, but should not lead one to forget that this social consciousness has been historically expressed and channelled in the forms of bourgeois political rule – and notably in its representative mechanisms and functions.

Electoral struggles, parliamentary debates and Party contests thus constitute the meeting-point of the two antagonistic poles. The centre of gravity in the class struggle is transposed and displaced to the level of presidential and parliamentary action in the existing legal-political framework – defusing and sublimating the direct action of working-class forces. Whether the divergencies and conflicts are resolved or not, there is factual agree- ment about the site of the confrontation: the legal terrain of political struggle at the summit, delimited by Consti- tution and custom. The interests of the antagonistic classes are concentrated, purified and refracted in this aseptic, ideal location, cut off from everyday struggles. 'Politics' is what happens to the Presidency, to the Senate, to the Intendancy (the Prefecture) and to the Municipal Coun- cils: it is the discussions and proceedings of assemblies. Hence everyone takes part in 'politics' at presidential, parliamentary and municipal election time (the rate of abstention is very low), but politics is the business of poli- ticians all the rest of the time. Parliamentary procedures go a long way towards softening the blows and absorbing the shocks. This is clearly visible today as all the bourgeois opposition's ancestral experience in the art of phagocy- tosis (which can be called the destruction by assimilation of a foreign body) is stretched to the limit in its efforts to fend off the impact of bills proposed in Parliament by the popular government. The bourgeoisie does not say no in principle to the projected nationalization of the American copper companies, or to the formation of popular tri- bunals at the local level: the Right opposition accepts the bill in general terms at its first reading, and then, in com- mittee after committee, in detailed observation and plenary discussion, it manages insensibly to blunt the edge – but without offering its flank to a frontal attack by popular forces. As a general rule, class clashes and con- flicts on the terrain of everyday struggles remain in- soluble until a parliamentary commission sent to the spot has given its decision. The issue of the confrontation is suspended until the adoption of the corresponding settle- ment or disposal, and the confrontation itself is ultimately transposed into a legal discussion or into behind-the- scenes negotiations on some proposed legislation. Repres- sive violence makes ink flow, before, if necessary, blood. It passes into the printed pages of the Official Journal from where it rebounds into everyday life. 'Our Trujillo has nearly always been the Law,' says Pablo Neruda, rightly. No doubt this legal dictatorship has proved susceptible to accidental damage (by breach as in the so-called one-hundred-day Socialist Republic of 1932) or to wear at the edges (by combination, as in the victorious popular coalitions of 1938 and 1946); no doubt it has proved susceptible to the infiltration, even in a completely capitalist regime, of advanced socialist legislation sanctioning or instituting various working-class conquests: in 1925, for example, after three years of discussion, the Senate finally adopted a Labour Code remarkable for the time, as well as a series of laws on the eight-hour day, on labour contracts, occupational accidents and trade-union law. But this is perhaps no more than the small change of the drama, the counter-part to the historical alienation which the supposedly representative institutions of 'popular sovereignty' ensured to perfection.

It is thus clear why the political *cursus honorum* was honourable for the representatives of the working class as well as for those of the big bourgeoisie. This is no historical degeneration but a state of fact characteristic of the workers' movement from the beginning. Nearly all the leading figures in the working-class parties have also been leading figures in the bourgeois Parliament. This has given rise to a style of action, a frame of mind, a certain kind of eloquence (the leader is generally a tribune) which would surprise an orthodox Leninism which, as we know – although it reckons it necessary to use all the tribunes made available to the workers by bourgeois freedoms – has never showed an excessive regard for what used to be called 'parliamentary cretinism'. Nevertheless, it is this terrain, sterile everywhere else, that the political understanding of the Chilean popular forces has been able to make a certain amount of use of and has had to fertilize to this day.

In this light, certain events and anecdotes seem less surprising. Thus, Luis Emilio Recabarren (1876–1925), first animator of revolutionary syndicalism and founder of the Communist Party, hero of the popular movement, if it has one, was twice elected deputy for Antofagasta and twice invalidated by an oligarchic Chamber as an agitator and an atheist, but he struggled obstinately to make his 'Right Honourable' colleagues go back on their decision and to force the doors of the Chamber of Deputies. In 1922, he returned from Moscow where he had gone as a delegate to the Fourth Congress of the Communist International, to resume his parliamentary mandate. In 1906, at the time of his first invalidation, he had heartily denounced the class character of the oligarchic Parliament, but he never questioned the legitimacy or utility of the institution itself. 'It is not we who bring this class division here with us in order to exacerbate it inside the Chamber,' he cried in his defence speech, addressing the Deputies, 'it is the Chamber which marks that division when it shows the poor man the door simply because he is poor. I may be mistaken, but I have the feeling that I shall not be dealt with justly. I should like to be wrong (*Ojala estuviera en error*), for if the Chamber pronounced in strict justice on my election, by that action alone it would build a saving bridge between those I call the oppressed and those who constitute a class apart and whom I dare describe as the oppressors. . . . I do not want to see brothers in a single nation plunge into an abyss of blood; but if that has to happen, we shall not be the guilty ones.' To take the initiative in a matter of direct action is neither a plausible nor even a legitimate hypothesis in Chile. '*Por la razón o la fuerza*' runs the motto on the national escutcheon: force, the last desperate resort, can only supplement the failures of reason. 'It is the people which elected me which will have to realize that here, in defiance of the Constitution and the Law, its clearly expressed will has been violated.' When Recabarren thus appealed for the application of the law, he was not just engaging in a tactical manoeuvre – catching the opponent in his own net – so much as expressing his nostalgic faith in the authentic rule of the Law, his inner conviction that he had common sense and justice on his side. Later, the Chilean

Party, in a period of retreat and sectarianism, continued to claim Recabarren as its own, but attempted to transcend his ideological heritage. In 1933, the South-American Bureau of the International sent it an open letter on this very theme, insisting on the Party's need to free itself of 'the ideological legacy of Recabarren, which constitutes a very serious political and organic obstacle to the Communist Party's assimilation of Marxism-Leninism, to its transformation into a really combative Party of the proletariat'. And the letter adds, 'Without wishing to underrate the great merits Recabarren won in the Chilean workers' movement, without forgetting that his revolutionary honesty and sincerity led him into the ranks of the Communist International, it is essential to bear in mind the fact that his ideology and political line did not go beyond those of "bourgeois democracy". His democratic demands, his faith in universal suffrage, his bourgeois patriotism, the foundation of our Party as in structure a Party of the social-reformist type, and its formation as a "federation" of purely electoral organizations, his ignorance and pure incomprehension of the worker-peasant revolution as a stage made necessary by the whole development, his abstract conception of the "social revolution" as a distant ideal and lastly the collaboration with the bourgeoisie which he justified as a "realistic" policy, all this ideological baggage left by Recabarren to the Chilean Communist Party as its inheritance has weighed heavily on its development.' However theoretically just this critique may be, it is still more obvious that the demands for the 'Bolshevization' of Communist Parties issued during the International's 'Third Period' had no practical success in Chile, leading the Party into a prolonged and sterile isolation from which it only emerged after the change of alliance and line before the Second World War represented by the Popular Front.

This brief backward glance was perhaps necessary for an understanding of the 'current moment' in Chile. Indeed, the popular government born on 4 November 1970 is the expression and historical product of the combined development, unique in Latin America, and maintained for good or ill to the present day, of the political forms of bourgeois democracy with a broad-based proletarian social movement. And Comrade President Salvador Allende is himself the living exemplar, almost the incarnation of this combination inscribed in the very dialectic of Chilean history; *Doctor* and *Compañero*; free-mason and Marxist; former President of the Senate of the Republic and immaculate socialist militant; bourgeois by formation and revolutionary by conviction: his roots in the provincial reality of his country (even more than in the capital) and a consistent internationalist – he is, in fact, as he likes to say himself, *criollo*, Chilean to his marrow. And if he were not this condensation of Chilean history, with all its occasionally disconcerting contrasts, he would certainly not have been in any position to attract to his name the first majority in the presidential elections, or to play the determinant part which is his at the present moment. It is no accident that Salvador Allende has been called by his compatriots – as head of State and of a legally constituted government – to throw a bridge between the society of the past and the society of the future, above, and in some sense *with the help of the contradictions* of the society of the present.

III

On the evening of 4 September 1970, the ruling class and imperialism discovered, without yet being able to believe it, that they had just suffered a crucial reverse. In fact, the electoral result was just one further episode in a much wider phenomenon: the general crisis of the dependent capitalist system and of its expression, the system of political rule. The increasing inability of the ruling groups to maintain their façade of legitimacy, to formalize the traditional compromise of interests, the accumulation in the urban centres of an unemployed and unskilled labour force which could not be absorbed by industrial production, the progressive denationalization of the economy and of the State itself, constant inflation, unemployment, a generalized housing crisis, direct action by the dispossessed peasants in the countryside, the revolutionary élan of student youth, the impact of liberation struggles in the neighbouring countries, the refusal of the masses, stirred by the programmes of 'popular promotion', to be manipulated by the government promoters – all resulted in a situation in which the hegemonic liberal framework, whose cracks revealed more and more of its authoritarian and vertical armature, was brought into question at every level. The *status quo* was stretched to its limit, and despite the formidable psychological campaign mounted by the Right, with unprecedented financial resources and the quasi-totality of the major means of communication at its disposal, two thirds of the electorate were agreed as to the necessity to replace it, to take the first steps along a revolutionary road, a 'personalist and communitarian' one for the Christian Democrats, a 'popular and socialist' one for the Left. The Christian Democrat candidate signalled in his programme and constantly repeated in his campaign 'the exhaustion of the old institutional system and of the capitalist and neo-capitalist economy, unable to produce wealth, to provide labour or to ensure the independence of the nation. Maintenance of the established order has become impossible. Institutional change is not just inevitable, it is desirable.' However programmatic and demagogic these statements may have been, they nonetheless reflected a level of consciousness shared by the majority of the country. For its part, the Popular Unity and its candidate conducted their electoral campaign without unnecessary stridency, but also without putting the flag away in their pockets, thus distinguishing themselves sharply from the 1964 campaign, conducted on the defensive in a more or less electoralist manner, by means of a certain lowering of the revolutionary combativity of the masses. The electoral campaign and victory in 1970 must be seen against the background, in the country, of the *tomas de fundos* and the invasion of unoccupied lands by the peasant unions, on the outskirts of the big towns, of the occupation by force of building land, the constitution of self-defence groups or autonomous community organizations in the *poblaciones-callampas*, the expropriation of banks by a few revolutionary commandos who engaged more and more in direct action, the wave of strikes and wage struggles throughout the country, and a generalized police repression which no longer recoiled from torture and the use of fire-arms. For many these were last-chance elections. An electoral victory for the authoritarian Right, however ill-gotten, would merely have exacerbated the contradictions to breaking-point, releasing an irreversible process of revolutionary armed struggle, thus made inevitable. In this situation there occurred one of those apparently irrational accidents of history which give it all its flavour: the ruling class, as we have seen, indulged in the expensive luxury of making an exhibition of its contradictions and ideological dramas, by allowing the existence beside the representative of Law, Order and Domestic Peace, of a convinced spokesman for structural reforms and the 'non-capitalist path of development', bolstered by John XXIII's encyclicals, by Maritain and Emmanuel Mounier, and in general well up in contemporary thought. With this breach open, the fortress was no longer impregnable, an incursion within the walls was possible. If Paris was well worth a mass, an electoral campaign was not too high a price to pay for the strategic heights of State power, for a foothold in a few strategic positions from which to continue the fight under better conditions. The relative failure of the Cuban *zafra* (sugar harvest) – the ten million one – just before the climax, might have given adverse propaganda a redoubtable weapon, but Fidel Castro, involved in the battle absolutely against his will, set things straight in an important television interview and, going over to the counter-offensive, declared that in these special circumstances, participation in the election campaign was essential and victory plausible. Which was no more than a realistic reading of the Chilean conjuncture.

In the 'longest fifty days' after 4 September, national and foreign counter-revolution played every trick at every level, as President Allende explains below in the conversations: economic sabotage, organized financial panic, terrorism, individual assassination, political manoeuvre and bargaining, selective assassination and plans for a *coup d'état*. Time was running out: decades of history cannot be changed in two months, a putschist or terrorist style cannot be improvised overnight. The big bourgeoisie and a large proportion of the military high command, caught napping, went crazy, despite the help of the CIA, and committed the appalling *faux pas* of the execution of the Army Commander-in-Chief, General Schneider. Finally, force of good habit and the weight of formal legalism proved stronger than the will and interests of the monopolistic bourgeoisie. Willy-nilly, the existing government officially plays the 'democratic' game whose prisoner it has found itself, so to speak. Has it not chosen the lesser of two evils? Was it not aware of the fact that a tactic of rejection would have led to the collapse of the institutional framework and of the State mechanisms of conciliation? Is this because the party in power, with its candidate still in the lists after he too had appealed to the anti-imperialist and anti-capitalist revolution, could not clearly and straightforwardly play the counter-revolutionary card without reneging – or unmasking itself? Whatever the answer, the walk on the edge of the precipice has ended well for the moment, for on 24 October 1970, given the signature of an 'Estatuto de Garantías Democráticas' by the Popular Unity, the Congress, in Plenary Session, confirmed the result of the election and President Allende was able to take office on 4 November 1970.

Criticized by some comrades as unnecessary and dangerous (MIR, the Socialist Party Youth), approved by almost all of the Popular Unity as inevitable and without much effect on the planned political mobilization of the masses, the signatures of this Statute of Guarantees, incorporated in the Constitution and aimed at ensuring the permanence of the organizational principles of liberal democracy – a permanence which the Popular Unity has not questioned at this stage anyway – obviously represents a tactical compromise. Thanks to this document, the Christian left, then represented by Radomiro Tomic, was able to neutralize the Right of the Party in power, and thus to fend off the manoeuvres of a more than reticent government apparatus – forcing it to come out in practice for an alliance with the popular left. But ultimately who has neutralized who? The question arises not just in the case of this compromise, for there have been and will be others of the same kind. Who has tied whose hands? When one uses the legal system of the bourgeois State, is one not simultaneously used by it – in practice? This is still only a question – and the reader will see the resolute optimism with which Comrade Allende answers it in this interview expressly intended for publication. This is doubtless already an assessment, but it is not intended to be an irresponsible criticism: the militant who is writing these lines in the status of a foreign observer remembers reading a chapter of *Left-Wing Communism* on the subject of compromises, and he does not share the opinion of those who regard them as unacceptable in general, independently of the prevailing balance of forces and special conditions at a given moment; no more than he shares the opinion of those who think it unworthy of a revolutionary to take part in elections and even suspicious that he should win them, whatever the circumstances and the country.

Such is the Chilean ambiguity – inevitable at the present, perhaps temporary, stage. Here, crystallized and revealed in a crucial conjuncture, we rediscover the reciprocal conditioning of the terms of the contradiction to which the long coexistence of bourgeois-democratic institutions and the rising popular movement has led. Each of the terms present, imbricated together, acts both as a limit and a sanction with respect to the other. The bourgeois State has been caught in the trap of its own ideological discourse: popular sovereignty – expressed by votes freely cast in the voting-booths by all citizens who can read and write – the cult of the majesty of the law, the respect of the most reactionary generals for the constitutionally established order, individual guarantees, the division of powers – each of them is a weapon which has escaped its control and flown back into the faces of the ruling class like a boomerang. There is something more than individually hypocritical behaviour in the fact, for example, that the leaders of the anti-popular plot were also those responsible for the maintenance of law and order, or even directly responsible for the inquiries into the plot – like General Valenzuela, head of the Santiago garrison and responsible for enforcing the curfew proclaimed in Santiago the day after the assassination of the Army Commander-in-Chief, who was in fact directly implicated in the plot, as were other high-ranking officers. In this improbable imbroglio, where the thief acted the policeman, and really was a policeman, the terrorist pleaded for public order and calm, the putschist for respect for the civil authorities, we can see vice pay homage to virtue, bourgeois class instinct to bourgeois ideology, the unconscious instinct of a panicking class to the strictures lastingly embodied in the 'collective ego' of the class. This double game is the player trapped in the rules of his own game – the rules he has himself imposed. But – a reciprocal determination, postponed and perhaps still ignored – in stumbling on its own trap, bourgeois democracy does not fall into it alone. It drags its antagonist in behind it. Not just because it can demand rent for its room from the temporary victor, stand before him as the creditor before the debtor, but, more subtly, by an effect of ideological impregnation and inhibition affecting the popular movement and its political officials from within. What then stands in the way is no longer bourgeois democracy directly in flesh and blood, but something worse: its ghost and memory. There can be no doubt that the methods used, the road taken in Chile, have proved their tactical effectiveness so far – thus confirming the Leninist principle that it is necessary to squeeze every possible use out of the limited instruments afforded to the exploited masses by democratic bourgeois republics. It remains to be seen how far the further development of the class struggle, the flourishing of mass initiative, the proletarian offensive, have not been mortgaged in advance, stunted at birth. What made the electoral victory possible also acts as a brake on its transformation into a complete victory. Could not what cleared the way to the government also close the road to power? Are not the preconditions for the genesis of the process also the preconditions for its blocking? Such, briefly condensed, are a few of the questions of a strategic kind already asked by many militants and leaders of the Popular Unity. In his own realistic and circumspect way, President Allende asks them too, and this foresight is encouraging. At any rate, the victories achieved up to now are considerable. It has already been possible in large measure to satisfy and consolidate the immediate interests of the toiling masses. The tasks of the moment are of a different kind, and it would be absurd to dispute the value of the present forward march on the pretext that no one can yet say where it will ultimately lead. But insofar as there is no more a good tactic without a good strategy than there is revolutionary practice without revolutionary theory, these questions can be held to be mobilizatory. Calls to vigilance have no chance of being heard – and everyone knows it – unless those that formulate them do not in their turn forget that there is no more a good revolutionary strategy without good tactics than there is theory without practice adapted to the really existing conditions.

IV

The popular government has not been idle since November 1970. In some two months, while in many parts of the country poor peasants and workers have freely seized the initiative, the government itself has gone over to the offensive on several fronts: economic, social and diplomatic. After the transfer of power, the big bourgeoisie resolved, by way of its mouthpiece *El Mercurio*, to resign itself to the inevitable. Turning over a new leaf, it declared its support for all 'measures of social justice' and exercised itself for a whole month, with a mixture of flattery and threats, to drive a wedge between Allende and the workers' parties, on the grounds that 'a President of the Republic must not be sectarian', i.e. because it is the duty of a socialist in power to forget his socialist condition. It soon regretted it. The *Compañero Presidente* proved the most 'irremediable' case of all, inflexible in the execution of his programme, breathing dynamism and daring into the popular movement, the pivot of its various components and the motor of the whole. At the end of the year, he gave the country an unexpected Christmas present: the nationalization of the banks, over the Congress's head, by means of the purchase of stock from small shareholders. This apparently anodyne measure is crucially important in Chile, for it cuts off at its source the economic power of the monopolistic bourgeoisie, taking from it its ability to arbitrate credits and loans, depriving it in the long term of its control of the means of production, communication and political propaganda. This decree marked the end of the armistice and the beginning of open hostilities: an acceleration in the reunification of the parties and move-ments of the Right, public appeals to subversion, the mobilization and harassment of the executive by all the centres of power in bourgeois hands (the legislature, the judiciary, the middle levels of the administration, not to speak of the big newspaper chains), the systematic absolution of those found guilty of sedition by the ordinary courts but cleared by the Supreme Court, armed resistance by the latifundists affected by the agrarian reform or the 'illegal' occupation of their lands, assassination attempts and plans for the same, not to speak of the planning of *coups d'état* conducted in conjunction with foreign repre-sentatives, which by definition remain secret. Conspiracy, too, is not idle.

This rhythm imprinted on governmental action (besides, surprise and speed are a political and technical necessity where nationalization is concerned) almost caught the popular masses off their guard, and they were found to be dangerously far behind their government. This advance, rapid initially, would not have been possible had not the State which President Allende and the Popular Unity inherited proved more malleable than expected. It is a corset, of course, but an astonishingly elastic one, stretchable to a certain degree. There were cracks in the existing legal-political armature, giving the new government a latitude in its interpretation of the texts, a marginal freedom of action which it was intelligent enough to use without delay. In fact, the short-lived Socialist Republic of 1932 had managed to promulgate certain orders-in-council in the economic and financial domain which it never had time to apply, and which subsequent regimes had purely and simply forgotten, not known about or ignored. The government has exhumed them from such profound oblivion that for several days the closest study by the lawyers in the service of the great industrial interests were unable to reveal what was going on, i.e. by virtue of which legal disposition it was possible to expropriate the businesses or factories of their clients. In fact, it was a very old order-in-council, clearly socialist in inspiration, authorizing, via a State organ, 'the intervention of the central power in all industries producing basic necessities which infringe on norms of functioning freely established by the administrative authorities'. The legislative arsenal can thus be turned round, up to a point, and used against the old legislators. In the same way, the presence of a certain number of traditional State or semi-State organs – the heritage of State capitalism – once they had been dusted off and put back to work, allowed the beginnings of economic control and planning. Finally, it is always possible to 'reform' or even change the Constitution by means of a plebiscite proposed by the President to the 'sovereign people' – an exceptional procedure which has not been used for forty years.

This resolves none of the fundamental problems – and the fundamental problem of a revolution, as we all know, is the problem of power. Constitutional law has its limits. The real settlement of accounts has merely been postponed. At present the existing State apparatus obviously does not correspond – or only does so very unevenly – to popular control. Hence the appearance of a new kind of dual power within, and at different levels of, the political machine. Understandably, the lack of control created a particularly delicate situation where the apparatuses of politico-military security are concerned. President Allende and his team took the initiative as to the individual security of the executive on the morning of 5 September by constituting their own protection squad, public but with no official standing, composed of tried revolutionary militants foreign to the 'Traditional Left', some of whom were still at the time working illegally, or were the victims of legal proceedings for their militant activities. Given the obvious dangers facing the President-elect and the deliberate failure of the government security organs, this was an imperious necessity. The spokesmen of the Right, with consummate pharisaism, appealing to Chilean traditions of *convivencia pacífica*, feigned astonishment and indignation, and stirred up a press campaign about it, but without success. The effrontery of the reactionary groups in secretly organizing, directly or indirectly, a series of attempts on Allende's life, while protesting against the security measures he was obliged to adopt, was really showing too little discretion. It is worth stressing that the MIR (Movement of the Revolutionary Left) has also put its own secret services at the disposition of the popular government and of the comrade President – who has publicly thanked them for it – and those services are remarkably efficient, for they have contributed to the prediction, revelation and sometimes prevention of various of the subversive operations, conducted by reaction with foreign assistance. Remember that, with the exception of the plan to assassinate the Army Commander-in-Chief, which was not tracked down in time, at least the MIR was able to denounce the plans for a *coup d'état* publicly after 4 September, presenting supporting proofs and details.

An experienced, pragmatic and intuitive tactician, Salvador Allende – and this is one of the most reassuring

revelations of the present time – has also demonstrated
that he is not retreating from his basic responsibilities.
In the event of a serious crisis, it seems we should not look
to him for hesitations and compromises. Without claiming
the role of a *caudillo*, as he explains himself in the interview, the fact is that he has won an important capital of
popular sympathy and support since his accession to the
Presidency. The Chilean people and its vanguard sectors
have indeed been able to watch the transformation – or
transfiguration, for those who believe in the grace of power
– of a candidate who did not have universal support,
even in his own ranks, into a full-blown, indefatigable and
daring *Compañero Presidente* who does not conceal his
fierce will not to yield an inch in the pursuit of the objectives set for him by the popular mandate. He will stick at
nothing. In a country – and more broadly, on a continent
– used to the demagogic promises of candidates whose big
words collapse in three months after they have obtained
power, the opposite experience of a respected but queried
candidate – seen from the outside he had the traits of the
best kind of Social-Democrat – who, once he has reached
the presidential chair, develops a revolutionary vocation,
evokes from many of his compatriots, and not only from
them, an astonishment which ranges from mere sympathy
to enthusiasm. Having said this about *Compañero* Allende,
his intentions and his own means of action are one thing,
the bureaucratic and governmental apparatus are another,
much slower, heavier and less disposed to take or reflect
the initiative. Although there is no visible sign of a fracture
in the Popular Unity despite all the enemy's manoeuvres
to produce one, we should remember that splits might
appear, that the working-class and Marxist parties are
not alone, and that the middle and lower strata of the
administration have not been replaced, by virtue of a law
passed *in extremis* under the old regime forbidding the
dismissal of the present officials. In other words, the
question of how the politico-administrative apparatus will
respond to the pressure and incitation of the President and
his team of leaders is still open. We are in no position to

answer it. However, the readers of the conversation below would do well to bear it in mind.

Similarly, it should not be forgotten that the process of popular struggles now in full swing is not always channelled by or even in control of the governmental apparatus. The struggle against the ruling class on the ground has its own dynamic and invents its own forms of action, which do not necessarily follow the route mapped out by the Popular Unity. It is often the unorganized or only just organized masses who themselves take the initiative, running ahead of or elbowing aside official control. Thus in the countryside, in the provinces of Cautín, Valdivia and the neighbouring regions, a Peasants' Revolutionary Movement is developing, and carrying out a series of *tomas de fundos* without first consulting the official functionaries of the agrarian reform at the provincial level, or else transforming the *Consejos Campesinos* at the communal level into organs of local power, choosing their representatives outside the existing unions and taking radical measures of self-defence, just in case. In the urban suburbs, spontaneous occupations of factories by the workers and the formation of management councils will probably soon cease to be isolated incidents. Inversely, the reactionary forces are taking the initiative in their turn, developing an offensive dynamic in the counter-attack, which also escapes governmental control. The reactionary counter-attack does not yet seem to have aroused an adequate response from the popular government, which lacks means of action, it is true. This unevenness is particularly sensitive on the level of mass communication, where the broadcasting apparatus controlled by the bourgeoisie reveals, day in day out, that the dynamics of communications are firmly in bourgeois hands. Much news, governmental measures, certain noteworthy decisions of the popular parties, such as voluntary summer labour, the departure of a mass of revolutionary students for the countryside, the new forms of democratic management in some centre of production, etc., are systematically distorted or purely and simply ignored. Meanwhile, every day the bourgeois parties publish immense advertisements in the mass-circulation press inciting Chileans to resist, reminding them that 'they are not alone'; they cover the walls with hostile or provocative slogans to which the 'Ramona Parra' and 'Elmo Catalan' brigades, i.e. the Communist and Socialist youth vanguards, find it hard to respond, for they only have a great spirit of self-sacrifice and a militant will on their side. Faced with the growing arrogance of the class enemy, the secondary contradictions within the revolutionary formations are in decline or moving into the background, to the profit of the common struggle against the main enemy. Even if divergences survive, this new unitary consciousness is the most positive and striking feature of the current situation. Unity of action between Communists and Socialists is an achieved fact; and the recent conversations between the leaderships of the Communists and the MIR after the serious incidents at the University of Concepción, conversations which would have been unthinkable only a few months ago, witness to the distance travelled in such a short space of time.

If, to sum up, I must characterize the relation of forces which prevails in Chile today, in January 1971, 'unstable equilibrium' would ultimately be the least incorrect expression. The apparent strength, the apparent almost nonchalant calm which reigns on the surface cannot efface the memory of the precariousness, the fragility of the present balance. In the last analysis, and until further notice, power grows out of the barrel of a gun, and the popular government does not have its own armed apparatus, its own institutions of defence on a national scale. It does have powerful mass organizations, the support of the workers, and constitutional legitimacy – an element worth underlining in Chile. Probably if the revolutionary dynamic led it out of the established legality, providing a pretext and the appearance of legitimacy to a *coup d'état*, the latter would not be long delayed. It is just as clear that if reaction, powerfully assisted from abroad, were to take the initiative, and itself break the *status quo*, becoming the first to launch into armed struggle, then the revolutionary river would leave its bed and in revenge burst all the banks in which it is confined today. The conditions would have come together for the qualitative leap, the process would change gear and perhaps nature, laying down the long-term bases for a new State: Chile would then really have '*changé de base*' as a line of the *Internationale* has it. Meanwhile, each of the existing camps sticks to its corner of the woods, waiting arms at the ready to see which will make the fatal blunder, which will break cover before the other.

For the moment, the popular camp has two weak points at which it might offer a target for an adverse stroke: first, a marked gap between class instinct and class consciousness, i.e. the fact that the political consciousness of the workers, or their consciousness of the long-term strategic interests of the proletariat and its allies in the struggle for hegemony, does not seem commensurate with their spontaneous will to defend their immediate vital interests. This dislocation is hardly surprising, since political consciousness is by definition the attribute of a vanguard; but in the long run, in a revolutionary period, the protection of the immediate interests of the workers and the improvement of their conditions of existence depend on their ability to transform a discrete, static, defensive position into a line of offensive aiming at the conquest and consolidation of political power as a nationally answerable class. And, a second dislocation – the duplication of the first at a higher stage – the gap between class organization (in quantity and quality) and the class consciousness itself. This is discernible at the union level (one quarter of the working class is unionized – and, as is to be expected, unionism is still steeped in the wage-claim mentality and 'economism' of the bad old days); and at the political level, the level of the parties, especially the Socialist Party whose qualities in the organization and mobilization of the masses and consistent discipline have not hitherto seemed commensurate with the political consciousness of its militants, nor with the objective responsibilities of its leaders in the conduct of the revolution. This phenomenon is still further underlined by the absorption of the available political cadres into the administrative and governmental apparatus at the local and national level, thus depleting the strictly political formations of leadership and cadres, leaving them anaemic and in no condition to perform their own tasks as vanguard organizations.

This cascade of gaps and dislocations leads finally to a certain lack of a *political leadership* capable of mobilizing and stimulating the mass movement at every level. *The governmental function cannot of itself stand in for the function of the political vanguard.* These are two instances which have to be distinguished in any revolutionary process whatsoever, two aspects of the action which must be coordinated but also kept separate, in order to prevent any confusion of the tasks of administrative management and political leadership, i.e. in order to avoid falling into manipulative bureaucratism or authoritarian oportunism. These imbalances, these hiatuses, these gaps, no doubt constitute the peculiarity of every revolutionary dynamic, its counter-part and even the surest sign of its existence – insofar as a revolutionary dynamic means the constant excess of tasks over the possibilities of their execution, of needs over resources. But these holes must be filled in bit by bit, they will not go away of their own accord; it is essential to keep up with the process of historical demands if the course of events is not to get too far ahead. This is not a question of individual abilities but of organizational abilities, i.e. in the last instance it is a question of the possession or non-possession of a correct conception of the class struggle to be conducted in a national-democratic phase, and this responsibility falls to the national political leadership and to no one else.

This relative failure of political leadership is not without its immediately practical and universally obvious effect: the divorce that exists today between the under-mobilization of the mass revolutionary forces and the virtual and actual over-mobilization of the minoritarian counter-revolutionary forces. The self-preservation instinct of a big bourgeoisie at bay can, without anyone realizing it, accumulate an unsuspected explosive charge, and release it openly at one stroke. The immediate fate contemporary history has reserved for those leaders and popular masses who have tended to believe that the essential has been won when they only had the ministries with them, is well known. The verbal and not merely verbal escalation of the big bourgeoisie, national and international, against the Chilean popular government is disquieting: it would be paradoxical, but also fatal, if in Chile imperialism and the monopolistic bourgeoisie managed to create a conscious vanguard, better prepared, better equipped, and more vigilant than the revolutionary vanguards existing today; and, as we know only too well, the history of contemporary revolutions, particularly in Latin America, has a taste for paradoxes.

But no one should sound the alarm without reason. The Chilean revolutionary process has every chance of following the route it has mapped out for itself, and those who have this responsibility are quite determined to take it to its conclusion. It is the interest and duty of all militants wherever they come from, to understand the special features of the road followed by the Chilean comrades, to follow them attentively along the road, to offer them a lucid and unreserved solidarity. This exceptional road – history, after all, progresses by zigzagging from exception to exception – has so far only been sketched in. It goes without saying, but it goes all the better if it is said, that the 'Chilean road' stops at the frontiers of Chile: as we shall see, Allende himself is concerned to set the limits. The basic road for the Latin-American revolution is armed people's struggle, to which each nation will in time give its own peculiar concrete forms. Tomorrow's Bolivian revolution, and the day after's Brazilian one, will undoubtedly have nothing in common with the current Chilean road, where the traffic does not seem very dangerous at first sight – which is what makes it all the more precarious. In fact, the Chilean vanguards, and all the revolutionary leaders, are conscious of the danger implied by the fact of having entered a profoundly new but apparently normal stage without a sharp turn, without a rupture, without a test, in alignment with the old routine. The danger in this situation is to approach and handle a virtually revolutionary and actually critical situation within the ideological schemata, methods of action and to some extent the reflexes inherited from earlier and outdated stages. If this were the case, the popular government would run the risk of falling behind a process it began itself, of losing control over it, and running straight into the ditch. 'We have made a revolution much greater than ourselves,' said Fidel Castro one day, in different circumstances. This is the disproportion of all historical enterprises, from the most trivial to the most serious: the actors are overtaken by the scope and the repercussions of their own action. But when the disproportion is too great, the actors are swept from the stage by the tempests they have sown behind them. It would be a pity if the forces which have won a first serious victory in Chile had unleashed a dynamic of class struggle which escaped them and was stronger than they were. If this dynamic is to be controlled and brought to a successful conclusion, it requires more from the popular officials, and from the people themselves, than what they can yet give in organization, leadership and defensive and counter-offensive ability (in the politico-military and not just the technical sense of the term). Popular Chile has aroused a cruel enemy which is now sleeping with one eye open and is ready to spring, to break its institutional trammels, to throw away its ethical inhibitions and to cast off its own restraints. A dangerous enemy because fear makes it aggressive. Can popular Chile face up to it? Can it do so in time? The answer to these questions does not just concern individuals, their personal gifts or qualities, but the organization of adequate collective responses. As far as Salvador Allende goes, as the reader will undoubtedly realize, he is ready to act commensurately with the consequences of his own choices.

In a word, however complex the concrete conditions in which it is posed, the ultimate alternative is as simple as can be: if the popular regime does not hold good come rain come shine, it will either softly slide into the quicksands of reformism or be removed by a *coup de force*. Comrade Allende shows no tendency either to be engulfed by half-measures or to offer his throat to the long knives of the enemy. The first solution remains: to hold fast. They say it is still a gamble. There is nothing to prevent us from hoping this gamble will be won.

Conversations with Allende

This interview took place in two parts, the first in Santiago and the second in Valparaiso, the seat of government in summer, the Popular Government having transferred to this town on 6 January, on which day President Allende held a mass meeting in front of the Valparaiso Administrative Building.

I

Debray: Comrade President, does a man change when he is in power?

Allende: Well, Régis, people always used to call me 'comrade Allende' and now they say 'comrade President'. Obviously, I'm aware of the responsibility that this implies.

Debray: Does a socialist militant change when he becomes Head of State?

Allende: No. I believe that the Head of State who is a socialist remains a socialist, but his actions must be consonant with reality.

Debray: It really is something new to find a socialist in power who still feels and acts as a socialist! There aren't all that many examples of this, comrade.

Allende: I know, unfortunately this is true. Nor are there many socialist parties which are Marxist in the true meaning of the term.

Debray: And if we could go back a little in time; you were one of the founders of the Socialist Party?

Allende: Yes, I was.

Debray: That was about '32...

Allende: 1933, to be exact.

Debray: What was the basis of your personal, political education? How did you come to join the Socialist Party?

Allende: I didn't join the Socialist Party, Régis – I am a founder, one of the founders of the Socialist Party.

Debray: My question would be: 'Why socialist rather than communist?'[1]*

Allende: Well now, when we founded the Socialist Party, the Communist Party already existed, but we analysed the situation in Chile, and we believed that there was a place for a Party which, while holding similar views in terms of philosophy and doctrine – a Marxist approach to the interpretation of history – would be a Party free of ties of an international nature. However, this did not mean that we would disavow proletarian internationalism.

Debray: I understand that there was a certain amount of sectarianism at the time . . .

Allende: You know quite well there was. The Communist Party was characteristically a closed, inward-looking party, and we believed that what was required was a party based, I repeat, on the same ideas, but which would have a much broader outlook, would be completely independent, and would adopt other tactics geared specifically to deal with the problems of Chile according to standards which are not dominated by international criteria.

Debray: I understand that the first socialist republic in Latin America lasted twelve days.

Allende: That's all . . .

Debray: and this was in Chile . . .

Allende: Yes, in '32.

Debray: Were you involved in it, or did the coup by Marmaduke Grove[2] have an influence on the founding of the Party?

Allende: Influence? It had a tremendous influence.

Debray: Did you have problems afterwards?

Allende: During that period before 1932, I was sent down from the University. It was during the time known as the Ibañez dictatorship,[3] which was certainly not typical of dictatorships in Latin American countries – in fact, one could say that it was a benign dictatorship, the outcome of a chaotic government and a chaotic economic situation,

* See notes on p. 131.

and, as generally happens, the student organizations had to stand up to the dictatorship. I took part in this, and for this reason I was sent down from the University and arrested.

Debray: Did they institute proceedings against you?

Allende: Yes. I was involved in five cases; I was tried by court-martial. When Marmaduke Grove's Socialist Republic fell, I was a houseman in a hospital in Valparaiso, and made a speech as a student leader in the Faculty of Law, and as a result, was arrested. Other members of my family were also put in prison, including my brother-in-law, Marmaduke Grove's brother, and one of my brothers who had virtually nothing at all to do with politics. As you can see, we had close family ties with Grove. On that occasion, we were tried by a court-martial which set us free. We were arrested again and put through another court-martial; then came the stage of the real trial. My father was unwell; he'd had a leg amputated and he had symptoms of gangrene in the other. In fact, he was dying, and my brother and I were allowed out of prison to go to see him. As a doctor, I realized just how serious his condition was. I was able to talk with him for a few minutes, and he managed to tell us that all he had to leave us was a clean, honest upbringing – he had no material wealth. He died the next day, and at his funeral I made the promise that I would dedicate my life to the social struggle, and I believe that I have fulfilled that promise.

Debray: There is something else I'm interested to know. I know that you are not a theoretician, but what one might call a firm conceptual foundation is apparent in your actions and speeches. So I wonder how you came to become a Marxist Leninist?

Allende: Well, the fact is that during my student days, I'm talking about '26 and '27 when I had just started reading medicine, we medical students were the most advanced.

Debray: Rather than the philosophers or 'humanists' in the Faculty of Letters?

Allende: Yes. The medical students were traditionally

the most advanced. At that time, we lived in a very humble district, we practically lived with the people, most of us were from the provinces and those of us living in the same hostel used to meet at night for readings of *Das Kapital*, and Lenin, and also Trotsky.

Debray: It is said that this is where you differed from the Communist party comrades, in that they didn't read Trotsky, I suppose.

Allende: Well, I believe that there are those who will tell you that the Communist Party would not read him, but there were no such barriers for us. I am well aware that there is no revolutionary action without revolutionary theory, but I am essentially a man of action. Since my student days I have always been in the front line of the struggle, and this has taught me a lot.

Debray: Yes, the University of Life, as they say; but books are another vital source of learning. A concrete question: Have you read Lenin's *State and Revolution*?

Allende: Yes, of course.

Debray: Good, because we'll probably discuss it a little later on.

Allende: In many of my speeches in Parliament, I have quoted passages from this work and earned criticism from the spokesmen of the reactionary press as a result. One such newspaper, *El Mercurio*, reproduced paragraphs from one of my speeches and from Lenin's book as an illustration of my intention, naturally, to 'suppress the bourgeois State'. I think that basic works like *State and Revolution* contain key ideas, but they can't be used as a Catechism.

Debray: I've always heard that you've had connections with freemasonry and yet you are a Marxist; you know at one time there was a serious dispute within the international workers' movement. For example, in France in the twenties, the freemasons were expelled from the Communist Party, which was then in its infancy. Do you see a contradiction between your supposed connections with freemasonry and your Marxist position, your class position?

Allende: First, Régis, let me remind you that the first Secretary General of the French Communist Party was a freemason.

Debray: Yes, yes ...

Allende: And that it was only by the time of the Third International that incompatibility between the two movements was established.

Debray: Yes.

Allende: Now, from a personal point of view, I have a masonic background. My grandfather, Dr Allende Padín was a Most Serene Grand Master of the Masonic Order in the nineteenth century, when being a freemason meant being involved in a struggle. The Masonic Lodges and the Lautaro Lodges⁴ were the corner stone of independence and the struggle against Spain.

Debray: Bolivar and Sucre were freemasons.

Allende: Exactly. So you can understand perfectly well that, with this kind of family tradition, and again, since the masonic movement fought for fundamental principles like Liberty, Equality and Fraternity, one can viably have such connections. Now I have maintained within the masonic movement that there cannot be equality in the capitalist régime, not even equality of opportunity, of course; that there cannot be fraternity while there is class exploitation, and that true liberty is a concrete and not an abstract notion. So you see I interpret the principles of freemasonry according to their true content. Now, I know perfectly well that there are countries where freemasonry could not be considered consistent with these principles.

Debray: Comrade President, you come from a fairly well-off family, one might say a bourgeois family ...

Allende: In orthodox terms, yes, my origins are bourgeois, but I would add that my family was not associated with the economically powerful sector of the bourgeoisie, since my parents were members of what are known as the liberal professions, as were my mother's family.

Debray: And where did they stand politically?

Allende: In Chile the struggle against conservatism was very violent during the last century, and it was fought out on a religious front. The conservatives opposed all progressive moves, such as the establishment of lay education. All my uncles and my father were Radical Party[5] militants at a time when being a radical meant that one held advanced views. My grandfather founded the first lay school in Chile and his political views earned him the nickname of 'Red Allende'.

Debray: And since then ...

Allende: Since then the family has maintained the tradition.

Debray: So family tradition could have influenced your upbringing. Do you remember any other kinds of influence?

Allende: When I was a boy of about fourteen or fifteen, I used to hang around the shop of a shoemaker, an anarchist called Juan Demarchi, to hear him talk and exchange views with him. That was in Valparaiso at the time when I was at grammar school. After the school day, I used to go and converse with this anarchist, who was a great influence on my life as a boy. He was sixty or perhaps sixty-three and he was quite happy to talk with me. He taught me how to play chess, he spoke to me of the things of life, and he lent me books ...

Debray: Which books?

Allende: All the essentially theoretical works, so to speak, like Bakunin, for example, but the most important thing was Demarchi's commentaries because I didn't have the temperament for reading in depth; he explained things to me with the simplicity and clarity that one finds in self-taught workers.

Debray: I see. And afterwards, you embarked on your political career. You were a Member of the Chamber of Deputies?

Allende: Yes, but first I began medical studies. I was a student leader and afterwards, in order to be able to work in the hospitals in Valparaiso, I had to take four examinations and although I was the only candidate, I was rejected because of what I had been as a student. I started to work as a pathology assistant, and that means that my first job was very hard and very dull. I had to carry out autopsies. Still in Valparaiso, in spite of my work, I engaged in militant activities and I was practically the founder of the Party in Valparaiso. I went into the hills and the suburbs, and out into the country . . .

Debray: So that when you return to Valparaiso, you feel at home there.

Allende: Look, I've always said this, my political career began in Valparaiso, I'm a native of this town, and I'm the first President from Valparaiso.

Debray: I understand that after being elected Deputy for Valparaiso, you became a Minister in the Popular Front[6] at a very early age.

Allende: Indeed. At thirty, I was a Minister under Pedro Aguirre Cerda. Look, that's Don Pedro in this photo; he was a man of great human qualities, a very kind man and interestingly enough, his contact with the people had the effect of bringing him round to an increasingly radical position. To begin with, he was the bourgeois-radical politician 'par excellence' and, in response to the loyalty and affection of the people, he was gradually transformed into a man of deeper conviction, much closer to the aspirations of the people, but he never ceased to be a Radical and never wished to be anything other than a Radical. That was at the time of the Popular Front; at that time, then, although it is true that there were the same Parties as today, the Radical Party, the party of the bourgeoisie, was the dominant party, and this is what makes the difference between the Popular Unity today and the Popular Front: in the Popular Unity, no party enjoys a position of supremacy, but there is a supreme class, the working class, and there is a Marxist Socialist President.

Debray: Afterwards, you continued in Congress and rose to become President of the Senate in the last years. How is it that a man from the petty bourgeoisie – with all those parliamentary, masonic, ideological and social ties – can carry out a consistently revolutionary line of action? Having been associated with many bourgeois institutions, the most representative of the régime into the bargain, how have you managed to become a leader of the masses, the prime mover of a process aimed at revolution.

Allende: I have often thought about this question. First, there is an intellectual commitment in youth, and later there is the real commitment with the people. I am a Party man and I have always worked with the masses. I am aware of being a grass roots Chilean politician and very close to the people. Remember, Régis, a great majority of revolutionary leaders have been drawn from the ranks of the middle and lower middle classes. Some, although they hadn't suffered the effects of exploitation personally, understood and felt what it was, they realized its implications and came down on the side of the exploited against the exploiters. I have always brought my political standpoint to bear on those institutions you have enumerated, and this standpoint has always been representative of the people's desires for social justice, and this is precisely what I'm doing now.

Debray: Good, let's move on to something else. Comrade President, you are now 62.

Allende: Yes, 62 well-filled years.

Debray: You belong to a generation, shall we say the generation of Betancourt, Haya de la Torre, Arevalo and their peers.[7] This generation is politically dead today. They are now a part of Latin American pre-history, and yet you are a central figure in its contemporary history, and will influence its future. Why were they left by the wayside, whereas you have continued to make progress?

Allende: Look, what you say is rather hard, but true enough. The truth is as follows: when it had been in existence for two or three years, the Socialist Party called a Conference of the popular parties of Latin America here in Chile. On that occasion, there were representatives of APRA[7] and other populist movements, but there was already a noticeable difference, because the Socialist Party was a Marxist party, and we were categorically anti-imperialist; at the time, APRA also claimed to be an anti-imperialist party. The truth is sad. What happened? When the popular parties, for instance 'Democratic

Action',[7] came to power in Venezuela, they lacked the positive approach required to make the necessary changes, there was no struggle to change the regime, the system – on the contrary they threw in their lot with imperialism. APRA, for example, has not come to power, but in its attempt to do so, it has modified, mitigated and changed its attitude to imperialism. As a result, these parties have been overtaken by history and do not represent or interpret the aspirations of the Latin-American peoples.

Debray: You knew many of these leaders personally.

Allende: Yes, all of them. Betancourt, for example, lived in Chile; I was Minister of Public Health under Don Pedro Aguirre Cerda when he came here in exile. We were quite good friends.

Debray: And you helped him while he was here?

Allende: We were friends. He lived opposite my house and we spoke to each other daily in those days. I should point out that he is a man of great mental agility, a great journalist and a magnificent speaker. He took part in a number of Socialist Party meetings.

Debray: There used to be a photograph of Betancourt here, I think?

Allende: Yes, but it hasn't been here for some years, since the Socialist Party broke with Democratic Action.

Debray: When was that?

Allende: It would be at least twelve or fifteen years ago.

Debray: When did the problem of imperialism become an issue for you? In other words, when did you become aware of your anti-imperialist vocation? The others never did become aware of theirs, or if they did, they abandoned them. When, then, did you enlist in the ranks of the anti-imperialists?

Allende: I think that when one has read Lenin, particularly *Imperialism, the Highest Stage of Capitalism*, one has a grasp of the theory. This issue of imperialism has a great deal of meaning in under-developed countries, particularly in Latin America. We Socialists have proclaimed that imperialism is our number one enemy, and we therefore gave and still give first priority to national liberation. The penetration and domination of foreign capital has increased to such an extent over the last few years that the so-called national bourgeoisie has virtually disappeared. The Socialist Party has a tradition of anti-imperialism which is bound up in history with the process known in this country as 'Socialist Revolution' which began on 4 June 1932.[2] Although it was only of short duration, this process had a profound influence on vanguard thought. In the 1932 revolutionaries' *Programme for Immediate Economic Action*, which I have at hand here, one finds this passage: 'Our privileged class has bartered our national patrimony and the misery of the people for the torpor of luxury and easy living provided by foreign capital.'

Debray: But was this anti-imperialism the driving force behind the Popular Front which emerged in 1936 and formed a government in 1938?

Allende: Look, we were aware that the Popular Front undoubtedly represented a great advance, because it marked the point at which the petty bourgeoisie took a share in the exercize of power and because it organized the working class into a Workers' Confederation, but at the same time we fully understood that economic dependence implied political subjection. And although it is true that the Popular Front was a step forward, it did not, and could not, bring about political liberation or complete sovereignty while the obstacle of economic dependence stood in the way. We were conscious that our activities in the Popular Front were a stage towards our ultimate aims, but we saw at every turn that the basic problems could not be solved. And why was this so? Because our real wealth was controlled by foreign capital. Thus it was that this practical experience strengthened our conviction that the essential struggle in the dependent or developing capitalist countries is the struggle against imperialism. This is the basis, the corner-stone of all other structural changes.

Debray: The emphasis was more on anti-fascism at the time of Pedro Aguirre Cerda.

Allende: But you must also remember the period in which we were living: the Spanish Civil War, the Second World War. . . . It is logical that, faced with the alternatives of bourgeois democracy or fascism, we opted for bourgeois democracy, like all the other working-class movements in the world.

Debray: And what was the reason for your breaking with all these people we have been discussing? What was the deciding factor? Why did you break with the Latin American leaders of your generation?

Allende: Because we realized that, in spite of having been in government, as in the case of Venezuela, these leaders lacked power, and they lacked power because they allowed foreign capital to continue to control their essential wealth. In other words, they did not seek to achieve economic independence for their countries.

Debray: Did not the Cuban revolution perhaps play its part in your breaking off with what we might term Latin American Social Democracy?

Allende: We had broken with APRA and Betancourt's party beforehand. Afterwards, undoubtedly, the Cuban revolution has had enormous influence, because we have seen still more clearly what imperialism is and how there are no frontiers when it is attempting to defend its interests. However, we also recall more than fifty landings of the Marines in Latin America. And you have to remember, for example, that Sandino[8] forms part of the social struggle of this Continent.

Debray: Even for Chileans? Does he come within Chilean historical consciousness?

Allende: He does and he always has. We, the popular parties have always remembered Sandino. Don't forget, also, that even Bolivar himself once said 'The United States seeks to submerge America in misery in the name of Liberty.'

Debray: This explains, then, why the Chilean Socialist Party has had nothing to do with the European Social Democrats for a long time.

Allende: Obviously. Nor does it have anything to do with certain self-styled socialist parties in Europe.

Debray: I believe, Comrade President, that you were one of the first politicians to arrive in Cuba after the victory.

Allende: Yes.

Debray: What was your first contact with the Cuban revolution?

Allende: I was in Venezuela when Betancourt took office, and it occurred to me to go to Cuba, since I had a few dollars to spare. Fidel Castro had already entered Havana. Fidel must have arrived on 6 January, if I remember correctly, or perhaps it was the 5th. I arrived on 20 January, at a very curious time. I was at my hotel, and that afternoon there was a parade which, for me, was not merely surprising, but quite simply incredible. This parade was headed by 200 Miami policemen, and in an open car, there were the Mayor of Miami and, I think, the Mayor of Havana. Next day, intending to take a plane to Chile, I met Carlos Rafael Rodriguez,[9] whom I had known in Chile. He asked me what I was doing there, and I replied: 'I came to see the Revolution, but since there is no such Revolution, I'm going. What kind of a Revolution is this going to be, with the Miami police in attendance?' He answered: 'You're making a mistake, Salvador. Stay here, speak to the leaders.' I said: 'No, no. I'm going.' But since he insisted so much, and since I knew Carlos Rafael, I said to him: 'Very well, but put me in contact with the leaders.' True enough, that afternoon I received a call from Aleyda, whom I didn't know, and hadn't heard of. She was Ché's secretary, but not yet his wife, and she said to me: 'Commandante Guevara is sending you his car, and will be waiting to meet you in the Cabaña barracks.' I arrived, and there was Ché. He was lying in a hammock, in an enormous room where I remember there was a bronze bedstead, but Ché was lying in the hammock. He was stripped to the waist, wearing trousers only, and when I arrived he was having a violent attack of asthma. He was using an inhaler, and waiting for him to recover, I sat down on the bed and said to him: 'Commandante' (Major), but he broke me off, saying: 'Look, Allende, I know perfectly well who you are. I heard two of your speeches during the '52 presidential campaign; one very good, and the other very bad. So we can talk in complete confidence, because I have a very clear opinion of who you are.' Afterwards, I came to appreciate Ché's intellectual quality, his human feeling, his continental vision and realistic understanding of the struggle of the people. He put me in touch with Raul Castro, and immediately afterwards I went to see Fidel. I remember it as though it were yesterday. He was at a cabinet meeting, and he brought me in and I attended part of the meeting. We had dinner, and then we went into a room with Fidel to talk. There were peasants playing chess and cards, lying on the floor, machine guns and all. We found a free corner of the room and talked for a long time. There I learned what this man Fidel Castro was like.

Debray: To summarize a little. Chile has its own road to Socialism, but you have followed the Cuban revolution closely during these twelve years. Evidently, there is no model, nothing which must be imitated mechanically, but what personal lesson did you learn from the Cuban revolution?

Allende: An extraordinary lesson. Firstly, that a united people, a people which is conscious of its historical objective, is an invincible people. Furthermore, when it has responsible leadership, when it has men who are able to interpret the people's will, to feel that the people *are* the government, and this is the case with Fidel and Ché . . .

Debray: You were talking about Fidel. How did the two of you become friends?

Allende: In fact, from the first moment, I was impressed by his immense intelligence – an incredible phenomenon that sweeps all before it like a sort of human cataract – and by his candour. And our friendship has been one in which there have been . . .

Debray: Differences of opinion?

Allende: Yes, fundamental and violent ones.

Debray: But always frank.

Allende: Always.

Debray: How did Fidel react when he heard of the victory of the Popular Unity in Chile?

Allende: He sent me a copy of *Granma*, the official organ of the Cuban revolution, which had the news of our electoral victory splashed across the front page. He had been at the offices of the newspaper waiting for the news from Chile, and he sent his congratulations on the front page proclaiming that ours was a victory against imperialism, signed it and had it signed by everyone around him. I keep it as a souvenir. He also called me the morning after the election to congratulate us.

Debray: Comrade President, you were talking about Ché. What was your personal contact with him?

Allende: As I have told you, the first time I went to Cuba, I met Ché, and since that moment I have had respect and affection for him and I think I can say that I was his friend. I have a portrait of him here which bears this dedication: 'To Carmen Paz, Beatriz and Maria Isabel, with the brotherly love of the Cuban revolution, and my own.' This shows you that he knew my daughters, and that as a family we felt affection and love for him, but there is something else I want to show you, something which has inestimable value for me. Something exceptional, which I guard as a treasure: *The Guerrilla War.* This copy was on Ché's desk; it must have been the second or third copy, since I imagine the first was given to Fidel. And here is a dedication which reads: 'To Salvador Allende, who is trying to obtain the same result by other means. Affectionately, Ché.' You will remember that afterwards, in 1961, an economic conference was held in Uruguay at the summer resort of Punta del Este at which the President of the United States, John Kennedy, launched his 'Alliance for Progress' programme. Ché was present at this meeting, and delivered his famous, prophetic, critique of this demagogical programme. At the same time, the Uruguayan anti-imperialist organizations invited me to take part in a meeting held in Montevideo as a counter to what was taking place at Punta del Este. Another of the people invited was Ché, and this was the occasion for us to meet again, this time in Uruguay. I gave two talks and Ché gave the closing speech to the anti-imperialist meeting, which was held in the Graduation Hall of the University of Montevideo. As we left after Ché's speech, he said to me: 'Salvador, let's go out separately, so that we don't offer a single target together if there's an assassination attempt.' We left separately. Afterwards we learned that there had been an attempt and that an unknown reactionary agent had fired on the crowd waiting for the political leaders to come out, killing a Uruguayan teacher. That evening, Ché invited me to the hotel where he was staying, to talk over dinner. On that occasion he introduced me to his mother, who was very dear to him. In the middle of the conversation, he told me a secret of the moment; the next day he was to travel to Buenos Aires privately, at the invitation of the Argentinian president of the day, the civilian, Arturo Frondizi. He made the journey, and the consequences of that private but obviously political meeting was the overthrowing of Frondizi. Shortly afterwards, the President of Brazil, Janio Quadros, was to be assassinated for decorating Ché as he passed through Brazil. The news of his assassination was a source of deep sadness to me. I shared in the mourning of thousands of my compatriots.

I should tell you, Régis, that I have known many men in the highest positions, but I have been struck by something which I have found in two men, which others lack. They are Ché Guevara and Chou En Lai. It is something in their eyes: both had an inner force, they both had firmness, and irony. I found that if I watched Commandante Guevara while we were talking, I knew what he was going to say before he opened his mouth. His eyes often betrayed tenderness and solitude. What always struck me was the fact that I saw his reply in his eyes before he uttered it.

Debray: After the assassination of Ché, during the military dictatorship in Bolivia, did you have the opportunity to demonstrate your solidarity at various levels with the revolutionary movement there?

Allende: As you know, I was President of the Senate when Ché's fellow-guerrillas arrived here. At the time, I went with them to Iquique and afterwards flew to Easter Island and Tahiti with them. There, Pombo, Benigno and Urbano signed the copy of *The Guerrilla War* which I had with me, with the following inscription: 'Comrade, with these few words we pay our homage to Ché, who offered you this book – his comrades in arms in the Bolivian guerrilla war.'

Debray: And it was courageous of you to do so, because I understand that the Right took full advantage of your gesture of solidarity to mount a hue and cry exclaiming on all sides: 'What is Allende doing? He's flying in the face of democratic principles.' On that occasion, you were obliged not only to defend yourself but to counter-attack against the bourgeoisie baying at your heels.

Allende: I was indeed, and during the ten days I was away from Chile, their main weapons against me were irony, sarcasm, mockery and ridicule. So I changed my position from one of being attacked to that of attacker. I met my detractors head on, and frankly, from that moment the attacks stopped. What's more, the plan was to censure me and kick me out of office as President of the Senate. They didn't dare try.[10]

Debray: When you assumed power officially at the National Stadium, where you gave your first political speech as President, there was a portrait of Commandante Guevara. You spoke of him as an example for Chilean youth. One question: why did you, with your different political attitudes, continue to support Ché Guevara, the Cuban revolution and Latin-American internationalism?

Allende: Because I believe, beyond any doubt, that there has rarely, if ever, been a man in the history of Latin America who had demonstrated such consistency in his ideas, such courage, such disinterestedness. Ché had everything, but he renounced everything to make the continental struggle possible. The answer to your question is contained in the dedication in Ché's book: 'For Allende, who is trying to obtain the same result by other means.' Of course there were differences, but they were differences of form, but the two positions were fundamentally similar, in fact the same.

Debray: Tactical differences?

Allende: Exactly. Each leader must make a concrete analysis of a concrete situation – this is the essence of Marxism. Thus, each country prepares its own tactics in the light of its own situation.

Debray: After the arrival of the Latin American guerrillas here, at the time when they managed to break the military blockade in Bolivia, I believe you went to Canada for a Vietnam solidarity conference, and you subsequently made a tour of revolutionary Asia.

Allende: I was invited to Korea and Vietnam.

Debray: Did this journey influence your political thought?

Allende: Of course. It did not modify my political thought but rather reinforced it. I was greatly impressed by the level reached by Korea in its economic development, knowing what the Korean war had meant, being aware that the armistice with Korea was the first signed by the American army, and knowing what conditions are like in South Korea today. But it was in Vietnam that the conviction I had felt, physically felt, in Cuba, was reaffirmed: a united, politically aware people, a people whose leaders have the moral fortitude, the prestige and the influence of Ho Chi Minh is an invincible people. I was impressed by the courage and vitality of these people. From my contacts with our comrades in South Vietnam, I learned a lesson in terms of clarity and breadth of political vision. The ten points of the National Liberation Front are an example of this breadth of vision. Their conception of the Revolutionary Front as a patriotic front interested me greatly.

Debray: As a matter of interest, before we begin talking

in strictly political terms, I believe you saw Ho Chi Minh a very short while before his death.

Allende: Well, I think I can claim to be one of the last Latin Americans, in fact one of the last politicians to have had the opportunity of meeting Ho Chi Minh, and this was one of the most interesting occasions of my life.

Debray: What was he like? What impression did he leave you with?

Allende: Firstly, he was taller than the average in Vietnam, an elderly man of great dignity, with eyes of diaphanous clarity, a man of unbelievable modesty, and yet this was Ho Chi Minh, whose history I knew. I knew what he had done: he had been a member of the French Communist Party, he was a founder member of the Communist Party of Indochina, he had been a leader of his people, yet he spoke with such simplicity... For example, during the time we were together, he spoke of 'his children' (I knew they called him 'Uncle Ho') with affection, with something which undoubtedly corresponded to what the people had learned to expect and understand in him. Personally, nothing impressed me more than Ho Chi Minh's attitude towards us, for example when he said to us: 'Thank you, comrades, thank you for having come from so far away, you have made a sacrifice to bring your moral support.' To hear this from Ho Chi Minh, from a man who had given his whole life to the struggle, from the victorious leader who had defeated the Japanese and the French, and was defeating the Americans...

Debray: Ho Chi Minh is a man of very simple deportment?

Allende: He behaved with an almost unbelievable simplicity. In his dealings with us, he was particularly friendly; this is illustrated by the fact that it was in Spanish that he said: 'Comrades, thank you.' Still in Spanish, he added: 'What a long way away your country is.' In my surprise, I asked him where he had learned Spanish and he told us that he had travelled along the coasts of Latin America in his days as a galley boy on merchant ships. This man, who, as an exile, had earned his living as a mere galley boy, welcomed us with such modesty in spite of his enormous political influence in the world. He was well aware of the situation of our countries.

Debray: You are shortly due to announce the resumption of diplomatic relations with the People's Republic of China?

Allende: Today, at midday, in Paris, Peking and Santiago, a communiqué re-establishing relations with the People's Republic of China will be issued.

Debray: This is a highly significant step for Latin America. Chile is the first country in the continent to ...

Allende: After Cuba, of course.

Debray: For you, and for the movement of Popular Unity, what significance is there in the resumption of diplomatic relations with the People's Republic of China?

Allende: It is of great significance, firstly, because Chile is exercizing its right as a sovereign state to enter into relations with any country in the world; furthermore, there is no doubt that, from the point of view of what relations with a country like China represents, it opens up wide horizons for us on a cultural, political and commercial front. This is why this step was part of the programme of the Popular Unity, because I must point out to you, Régis, that our relations with Cuba, our relations with China (and there is a Korean Commercial Delegation here, and a Vietnamese one is coming), and the resumption of relations with the German Democratic Republic – these are achievements of the people, things that the people have made possible through their political awareness. This is not a present from us, the leaders. No, this is the fruit of years of struggle; for many years, the people have been demanding it, and this is proof of the level of political awareness here.

Debray: You have followed the course of recent events in China? I am referring to the Cultural Revolution.

Allende: Yes.

Debray: What significance does this have for you?

Allende: It would perhaps be pedantic on my part to try to say much about the Chinese Cultural Revolution.

From Chile, it is difficult to obtain an understanding of events in such a distant country. By the time information on this phenomenon, whose importance I do not underestimate, has reached Chile, it has been distorted and is no longer reliable. Therefore, I cannot claim to have got to the root of the phenomenon. I understand that Mao Tse-tung, as a revolutionary, has sought to destroy the elements that were paralysing and neutralizing the Revolution. Such elements must be singled out and eliminated. This, for me, is the significance of the Cultural Revolution.

Debray: In the last analysis, it is the masses who decide and the Party cannot go over their heads. This could be a fact of universal significance. I would like, if I may, Comrade President, to ask you one final question of a personal nature before discussing the current Chilean situation itself. You have often been a candidate for the Presidency of the Republic, but we are well aware that the Presidency does not represent an end in itself for you, but rather a means towards an end, shall we say another battle front to be used for your revolutionary ends. What is your position as President like in practice? Doesn't it have a paralysing effect; doesn't the formal aspect, the protocol, stifle effective action? Don't you feel that you are gradually becoming institutionalized?

Allende: Of course, the danger exists, but since we are aware of it, we try to eradicate it. Moreover, contact with the people, the masses; the consciousness of the peasants and coal miners; dialogue with the trade union representatives or squatters*; being in touch with their preoccupations, hearing their criticisms of what we are doing – this provides us with a greater stimulus in the revolutionary task on which we are engaged. If I were to allow myself to live the traditional life of a President, if I were not fully aware that becoming President is not a question of maintaining the *status quo* but a matter of making revolutionary changes, then perhaps I would feel inhibited by the formal conventions by which a traditional President

* *Pobladores*: shanty-town dwellers who have built on land to which they have no legal right (Trans.).

is bound. In anything connected with protocol, one can adopt new standards ranging from very elementary to very important matters. Nowadays, nobody wears tails for official ceremonies, nor do we use the Palace carriages. We have broken with the traditional conception of protocol. Why? Because when we address the people, we are putting our points of view to them, we are showing them what we stand for and where we are going. We do not offer empty phrases. It is a question of using diplomatic channels to bring home the facts of the situations with which we are confronted.

Debray: Let us now discuss the current situation in Chile. With Frei, reformism ended, it failed. With you in government, the Chilean people has chosen the road of revolution, but what is revolution? It is the transfer of power from one class to another. Revolution is the destruction of the machinery of the bourgeois State and the replacement of it by another, and none of this has happened here. What is happening then?

Allende: Excuse me, comrade, let's deal with the question in stages. Indeed, the people of Chile chose the road of revolution and we have not forgotten a fundamental principle of Marxism: the class struggle. During the electoral campaign we said that the purpose of our struggle was to change the régime, the system. That we sought to form a government in order to obtain the power to carry out the revolutionary transformation which Chile needs, to break the nation's economic, political, cultural and trade union dependency. And you say nothing has happened here? What country do you think you're in? But wait, look Régis. During the few months we've been in power, we've . . .

Debray: Done a lot of things.

Allende: Yes, we've done quite a lot. We have been able to do them because behind them there is the tradition of the Chilean working class which began its struggle at the beginning of the last century and emerged as a force to be reckoned with during this century. In 1909, the Federación Obrera (Workers' Federation) was founded in

Chile. It was originally a mutual aid organization, but in 1919, with a new programme, it set itself the objective of abolishing the capitalist régime. You must take into account the fighting tradition of the Chilean working class. There have been stages in its development when its interests have coincided with those of the petty bourgeoisie. You must also remember that in Chile there are parties, drawn from the masses, which genuinely represent the ideology of the working class. At present, the people are in government, and from this position they are struggling to gain power through the programme of the Popular Unity, implemented by a vanguard composed of two Marxist parties, the Socialists and the Communists, two parties of bourgeois popular extraction, the Radicals and the Social Democrats, and two movements of similar background, the Christian Movement (MAPU) and the Independent Popular Alliance (API).[11] In addition, the government can count on the support of the working class organized through the Single Workers' Union.[12] This is a working-class government because the predominant ideology is that of the working class. The interests of the exploiting class are not represented in the Government – on the contrary, there are wage-earners in the Cabinet, four of them workmen. Through this Government, the majority of the people will replace the minority which has been in power until now. As for the bourgeois State at the present moment, we are seeking to overcome it. To overthrow it!

Debray: But bourgeois democracy remains intact here. You, in fact, hold the executive power.

Allende: Yes.

Debray: But not legislative or judicial power; nor the apparatus of police power. Legality, the Institutions, these were not the work of the proletariat; the bourgeoisie formulated the Constitution to suit its own ends.

Allende: Of course, but listen for a moment, we'll get to that later. What did we say during the electoral campaign? We said that if it was difficult, although not impossible, to win the election, the stage between victory and taking Government was going to be very difficult, and it would be yet more difficult to build, because we were blazing a new trail, for Chile, opened by Chileans, for our country. And we said that we would take advantage of what openings there are in the present Constitution to open the way to the new Constitution, the people's Constitution. Why? Because in Chile we can do it. If we put forward a bill and Congress rejects it, we invoke the plebiscite. I'll give you an example: we propose that there should be no longer two houses in Congress,[13] the proposal is rejected by Congress, we hold a referendum and win. Hence the end of the two house system, and we now have to go to a single house, as we had proposed. And who are the people going to elect to this house? Its representatives, I would presume. If we put into practice what we have said, and carry on with what we are doing ...

Debray: And one has to admit one thing, comrade. Since the elections, you have won many votes, or rather supporters and allies among the people.

Allende: I believe so.

Debray: I'm told so by a number of people. The Popular Unity is broadening its support socially. It is interesting that instead of the traditional loss of support of a 'Government of the left' once it has got into power, in this case, support is growing. Do you envisage a time when there will be a genuinely popular revolutionary majority?

Allende. Look. We haven't been around long enough to show a loss of support, but of one thing I am sure, yes, and that is that our adversaries on the right, and even a lot of people on the left, mind you, first of all didn't believe we would win, and then they didn't think we would carry out what we had said we'd do. Then, we hit back hard at reaction. Persistently. We hit them, they don't recover, and we let them have it again. For example, the Constitutional Reform for nationalizing copper. Think of the CUT-Government agreement; think of the creation of the National Peasant Council, the expropriation of an

important textile company in Concepción, the nationalization of steel, the nationalization of coal, the Bill to
nationalize the banks. Now then, Régis, are we or are we
not seeking the path which leads to Socialism. No wonder
the people are behind us, supporting us. Look, I'm going
to Valparaiso this afternoon. Come with me.

Debray: With pleasure.

Allende: There's a public meeting, and you'll be able to
see how the people respond.

Debray: I know you are on exceptionally good terms
with the masses.

Allende: The people have grasped the importance of the
measures we have taken. In addition to the basic socio-
economic measures, we had an immediate programme for
improving the living conditions of the workers. We are
the first Government to fulfil its election promises. For
example, a major problem is malnutrition in infants. We
proposed to give half a litre of free milk to every child,
and this we are doing. We have eliminated the various
types of loaf of bread and enforced a standard size to
eliminate price juggling. Bread is part of the staple diet
of the people. Chile is a country which suffers from high
inflation – in 1969 it was one of the ten countries with the
highest rates of inflation – and readjustment of incomes,
on an annual basis at least, applicable to salary and wage
earners has to be introduced. The Popular Front Government, which inherited a rate of inflation of 35%, must
regulate incomes by law in 1971. This time the Bill we
have submitted to Congress is not a traditional one; the
object is to facilitate economic development. Not only are
we seeking to restore the lost purchasing power to the
working class, but we are aiming to stimulate demand
in order to accelerate internal economic development,
which was impeded by the bourgeois Christian Democrat
Government. Don't be frightened, we haven't forgotten
that we are making our way towards Socialism.

Debray: No. I realize that there are special circumstances in Chile and that it was necessary to proceed in
this way. The important thing is that things are moving

and a lot of progress has been made in two months. But I come back to my earlier question, comrade Allende; the workers behind you have voted you into office, but if I ask you how and when you are going to win real power, what is your answer?

Allende: My answer is that we shall have real power when copper and steel are under our control, when salt-petre is genuinely under our control, when we have put far-reaching Land Reform measures into effect, when we control imports and exports through the State, when we have collectivized a major portion of our national production. I say 'a major portion' because in our programme we announced frankly to the nation that there would be three sectors in the economy: nationalized industry, a mixed sector and the private sector. Now then, if these things – affirming our national sovereignty, recovering our basic wealth and attacking monopolies – do not lead to Socialism, I don't know what does. But there will be no further doubt as to whether we hold real power as soon as Chile becomes an economically independent country. Hence our basic, most vital, principle is one of anti-imperialism, as a first step towards the making of structural changes. Hence the most important bill we have to get through is the one to nationalize copper, Chile's fundamental source of wealth. What do you think?

Debray: Yes, it is. Undoubtedly, at the moment the main emphasis of your activities, the main battle front, is concerned with the economic infrastructure. To understand this, one only has to remember that this Continent has a long history of pseudo-socialist phraseology and populist demagogy which is renowned for its failure to deal effectively with the economic and financial bases on which the capitalist system is built. But the problem of Socialism cannot be simplified into a problem of ownership of means of production. You, comrade President, know better than I that nationalization in itself means little. It remains to be seen whether nationalization can be converted from a mere legislative act on the part of the State into a genuine process of socialization, real and effective control and management by the State – and this does not only depend on the will, but also on the general development of productive resources. The class nature of the State which nationalizes the means of production remains to be seen. It remains to be seen whether the relationships of power and authority between the men in those centres of production actually change once the workers have theoretically become the owners of the factories or the land where they work. You know Lenin's slogan: 'Socialism equals electrification plus the Soviets.' We could change the terms which don't apply to the Chile of today, but could we now discuss the 'Soviet' as well as the 'electrification' aspect, 'men' as well as 'things' . . .?

Allende: It is true that if one views the problem from the point of view of building the socialist society, once one has got over the decisive and very absorbing current problems of the Constitution and securing power for the people and the destruction of the economic bases of monopolistic capitalism, other problems begin to come to the fore. As you rightly point out, the problems of the control and growth of socialized productive resources and the new relationships between the men inside and outside production need to be dealt with. With regard to the first problem, you have to realize that one of the outstanding features of Chilean capitalism has been its strongly monopolistic character, although the productive structure on which it is based is quite weak. In industry, for example, less than 3% of our companies control more than half of our industrial resources: capital, volume of sales, profits, etc. . . Into the bargain, most of these firms, and most of those in other sectors, are dominated by a clique of no more than fifty industrial, commercial and financial groups. Well now, in Chile there is a long tradition of State intervention in economic activities, along capitalist lines of course. Any number of State-controlled undertakings, control of prices and supplies, partial or total control of foreign trade, etc. . . Thus, from this point of view, we find ourselves already approaching socialism through the ante-chamber of State monopolies and State capitalism. The essential thing is to change the socio-economic content of their management. To this end, we must expropriate the means of production which are still in private hands. To quite some extent, the infrastructure for productive resources and their control has been prepared.

Debray: But how will the new social relationship be established in this context?

Allende: As for relations between men, and the possible and desirable forms they may take, you are well aware that this subject has been discussed fully in the Socialist countries and that various standards have been adopted or tried out in practice. We are aware that the subject has not been closed, and without any doubt no one can claim dogmatically that they have 'found *the* solution'; we must draw upon our own experience, which in turn springs from the historical and social contradictions which have given rise to our socialist revolution. Of course, there are certain elements which are derived from the experience of other countries, which are more or less common to many of them: the creation of a new system of values in which the social character of human activity is underlined; reassessment of work as the essential human function; reduction of the impulses stimulating self-interest and individualism to a minimum. In the meantime, we can show that in practice the management of the concerns in which the State has intervened, or which it has expropriated, is now in the hands of Workers' Committees in each factory, headed by a manager appointed by the State. Their objective is no longer to make profits, but to meet the present and future needs of the people. As State ownership progresses, the planned means towards this end will be strengthened.

Debray: Comrade President, as a Marxist, you are well aware that no social class relinquishes power with good grace. We know that the people are not yet in power, but at least they are in office and to an outside observer it would seem that the change of Government took place in a very civilized and stylish manner. For example, I recently came across a copy of *Le Monde* in which I read, and I quote: 'For the first time in history, in Chile, Marxism is settling comfortably into the seat hitherto occupied by the bourgeois democrats.' Have things really been as easy as that? Have the gentlemen of the previous government really been as benevolent as all that towards the Government of Popular Unity?

Allende: I think there is a slightly distorted impression with regard to the resistance put up by the reactionaries to our succeeding in office. During the elections, they used every means available. Already in 1958 and 1964, they used lies, calumny and slander, dirty anti-communism, and in 1970, it was worse still. Well, they were wrong, not us. Such was their insolence that they thought they could win a three horse race. We won, but I must tell you, Régis – as I told the people, and as I was saying to you only a moment ago – it is difficult, but not impossible to win. Let me enlarge on this. We beat them by playing to their own rules. Our tactics were right, theirs were wrong. But I said at the time to the people: 'between 3 September and 4 November, Chile is going to feel like a football being kicked about by a Pele.' I expressed it like that so that the people could understand. *Le Monde* can say what it likes, but the facts in Chile were very different. From 4 September, the day on which I was elected President, till 3 November, the date on which I assumed office, I was not a man preparing to take over government, I felt more like a Director of Public Prosecutions.

Debray: But wasn't this job being done by someone from the previous Government?

Allende: Obviously, there was a Director of Public Prosecutions, but he had no interest in protecting the legal system which had conferred power on the Popular Unity. I warned this official, in good time, that a powerful textile industrialist had arranged for a bomb to be planted in his house in order to justify his leaving Chile with his money. The Chief of Police did nothing, and the bomb went off. Following our public protests and denouncements, the people implicated in this plot were arrested but the magistrate at the hearing set them free. They were mem-

bers of an ultra-reactionary political party, and they fled
the country. To help you understand this case, I should
point out that the first phase of this conspiracy on the
part of the enemies of Chile and its working class was a
campaign of alarmism designed to provoke panic in the
weaker sectors. The plan was that the fear instilled in our
weaker friends would spread and thus the next phase of
the plot could be put in train. I should add that this was
an organized conspiracy. Some of the conspirators made
some spectacular withdrawals from the banks, which
caused thousands of anxious citizens to draw their money
from the savings centres. The radio and press media spoke
in terms of the 'danger of Marxism', and the Minister of
Finance of the outgoing Government, instead of pacifying
those who were really worried by the campaign of alarmist
rumours, made a speech calculated to intensify the false
impression of chaos in the country. It was in this climate
that the second phase of the conspiracy was put into effect
– the bombing of public buildings and monuments, private
houses, offices, etc... Santiago's international airport was
on the point of being blown up.

Debray: Was this the first time such a situation had
existed in Chile?

Allende: But I've only told you the beginning of it.
They invented an organization which was supposed to be
responsible for the attacks; of course, it was described as
a revolutionary organization. The idea was to blame us
for the attacks. Members of the reactionary conspiracy
assassinated a uniformed policeman who was on guard
duty in a public building, and fired on another, who was
seriously wounded; he was on patrol at the entrance of a
foreign embassy. Two attempts were made on my life, but
failed thanks to the watchfulness of my personal guard of
revolutionary comrades.

Debray: And the Commander-in-Chief of the Army was
killed instead?

Allende: I was the intended victim. Tragically, they
killed the Commander-in-Chief of the Army because he
refused to take part in the reactionary conspiracy. The

conspirators hoped that the crime would be laid at the door of the political body I represented and that the armed forces, particularly the army, would react politically to prevent the decision of the people bringing us into office from being implemented. However, Army Intelligence found evidence which points to the origins of the assassins.

Debray: Did you feel there was a possibility of civil war? Could you see it coming? Were you afraid of it? How close were you?

Allende: Yes, the assassination of General René Schneider[14] proved how close we were. Had the reactionaries kidnapped the Commander-in-Chief of the Army, we would undoubtedly have been on the verge of civil war. They continued to provoke the armed forces in an attempt to get them to overthrow Congress. Don't forget that the criminal attack occurred forty-eight hours before Parliament met for a Plenary Session to sanction the presidential election results constitutionally. By this stage, the Popular Unity already had the Parliamentary votes to ratify the victory won in the election of 4 September, so that the unconstitutional manoeuvre which consisted of a letter sent by the defeated presidential candidate, Jorge Alessandri,[15] was forestalled. Having lost all possibility of defeating the Popular Unity legally, the conspirators went outside bourgeois law. What could the people do? We had to defend ourselves.

Debray: So the outward appearance of the bourgeoisie conducting a clean, democratic campaign does not fit the facts? Was there resistance against allowing you to assume the Presidency?

Allende: Probably, if not on a personal level, certainly from the existing régime as a whole. It stands to reason that it should be so – you, as a Marxist, know that as well as I do, Régis.

Debray: The reactionaries defended to the last; they exhausted every possibility . . .

Allende: Not every possibility, no, because they are still active . . .

Debray: Yes, this is to be expected. This leads me to a

question which well . . . may or may not be of interest. Why for the first time, as President of Chile, have you been obliged to resort to a personal political guard?

Allende: I turned for protection, as you say, to a group of comrades because I had no confidence in the Political Police of the bourgeoisie. I knew that the Director of Public Prosecutions was doing nothing to find the people responsible for the attack. Worse still, I was quite sure that he knew who one of them was. So I had to seek other means of safety, not for my own life, but for what I represented. This is why I am accompanied by these young comrades, each one a proven revolutionary, each one a militant volunteer, and they take care of my personal safety.

Debray: Didn't you feel protected by the Government before?

Allende: No. As I have told you, the top police officials were political puppets.

Debray: Is it true that there was an attack on members of your family in front of your house and that you had to come out to defend them with a gun in your hand because the Government had 'forgotten' to allocate Carabineros to guard you?

Allende: What I can say is that I had every confidence as to how the armed forces would behave. As for the Carabineros, you have to remember that they take their orders from the Government, through the Minister of the Interior. Also, at the time of one of the attacks on my home, there was only one policeman on guard at the door, and he didn't have orders to shoot. The gang that attacked was large, so I had to come out shooting to frighten them away.

Debray: What significance is there for you in the fact that, in order to get through the first phases of the so-called 'peaceful process', you had to resort to men and methods who have little to do with this line to ensure your personal safety?

Allende: It's a question of form; the objective is the same, even if the tactics are different. You know that today in Uruguay, the Tupamaros, who have nothing to do with the Socialist Party or the Communist Party are working towards the possibility of a broad-based unity in Uruguay. You also know that here there was almost a confrontation between the MIR and the Communist Party as a result of the university elections in Concepción,[16] and I stepped in and helped to stop it happening.

Debray: Precisely, and since this is your role, that of unifier of the parties of the left, catalyst of the popular forces, it occurs to one that your enemies inside and outside the country would have good reason to eliminate you at present. If this came about, what do you think would happen?

Allende: The notion that history is based on personalities is a common delusion among the bourgeois class. The reactionary forces encourage this belief, and try to turn it to their political advantage; it is one of their favourite tactics to resort to methods of this kind, but we have an answer to this in the awareness of the people. I believe that although this would apparently be the easiest course for the reactionaries, the consequences of such an act would in fact be even worse for them. This is not to say that my presence contains them, but, without a shadow of doubt, if this happened, it would be quite evident that the reactionaries are no longer prepared to play to the rules which they themselves invented. They can lay no accusations at my door – all the civil liberties have been maintained: freedom to hold meetings, freedom of opinion, freedom of the press, etc. . . . The social process is not going to disappear because one of its leaders disappears. It may be delayed or prolonged, but in the long run, it can't be stopped. In the case of Chile, if they assassinate me, the people will carry on, they will follow their course, with the difference perhaps that things will be much harder, much more violent, because it would be a very clear and objective lesson for the masses showing them that these people stop at nothing. And I have accounted for this possibility; I don't lay myself open to it, I don't offer opportunities, but at the same time, I don't think about the possibility of this happening all the time.

Debray: If they go outside the law, will you also go outside the law? If they hit out, will you hit back?

Allende: If they deal us an illegal blow? We'll return it a hundredfold, you can be sure of that.

Debray: One thing has surprised me: this is the relative absence of mobilization of the people. Certainly, there was a great mobilization of the people at the time of the elections, but it seems to me that it has now fallen off. My question is therefore: how do you propose to transform this electoral mass into a revolutionary mass?

Allende: Look, before answering, I want to tell you that what you say is true, but only to a certain degree. The lines of communication with the people are the Parties of the masses in the Popular Unity, which are revolutionary in character. Furthermore, I have not cut my direct links with the people. On the contrary, I have gone out to meet and talk with squatters, miners, and agricultural workers in the places where they live and work. In addition, we have communications media at our disposal, they are not all in the hands of the enemy. We are not as completely devoid of media as all that.

Debray: Won't there be a risk of a sort of benign paternalism creeping into the conduct of the process of government. I don't mean to say a 'caudillo' system, but a situation in which you rain decrees on a people which accepts them, which understands them broadly speaking, but which has not asked for them, has not called for them. You say: 'the people are the Government', 'the people are in La Moneda'. How do you intend to turn these slogans into reality?

Allende: Firstly, you have to know the situation in Chile; you know that the struggle of the revolutionary Parties is a struggle which is being fought over the decades. You must know that what is happening in Chile is a phenomenon which is unique in the world – the concerted action of the Socialist and Communist Parties, which are both Marxist parties; this union has lasted over fifteen years, and neither party has lost any of its inherent characteristics. And you cannot forget that the six political parties which make up the Popular Unity have formulated a common programme, a programme which marks out the road of Socialism. The process in Chile is neither paternalistic nor charismatic. On the personal level, I have said it before and I repeat – I am not a Messiah, nor am I a caudillo. We know that popular power is built from the base upwards. Indeed, you cannot forget that the grass-roots organizations of the Popular Unity are its Committees responsible for watching over the implementation of the programme.

Debray: But I understand that these Committees, born of the heat of the pre-election struggle, have lost some of their fire since the victory.

Allende: Yes, there's some truth in that, but this is so because they have had to cope with a very wide range of new responsibilities. For example, take the Committees (CUP)[17] engaged in the distribution of the half-litre of milk; the Committees (CUP) involved in land questions – the problems of estates, of Land Reform. Just imagine, at this particular time, we have more than 65 farming properties which have been taken over by the CORA (Land Reform Corporation) and we have had to put in factors, we've had to pick our men for these jobs, and the Committees (CUP) in these regions and on these estates are taking part in this. Don't forget that we have just expropriated possibly the biggest estate in the world – 528,000 hectares. But I agree with you, the people's share in all this should be more active, better organized.

Debray: I see what is perhaps an anomaly here. At the top, one finds great dedication and great revolutionary fervour, where at a lower level, one sees an energy among the dispossessed rural masses, of the homeless, but it is disorganized and, at times, chaotic. How do you intend to establish an organized relationship between this pressure of the masses from below and the people responsible for running the country?

Allende: The lines of communication are there; they

are the Parties, the trade associations, the people's organizations. Besides, you always have this imbalance in the initial stages of a revolutionary process. Remember the lack of coherent organization at the time of the Land Reform in the Soviet Union, remember Cuba at the beginning.

Debray: Exactly. And on the subject of Cuba, I notice something which everybody notices when they arrive here: in Chile there is a tradition, a patrimony of political awareness among the people, of a kind that Cuba never had in '59, for reasons which are easily explained. How do you intend to turn these inherent advantages to good effect?

Allende: It would be a crime if we didn't turn them to good effect; this tradition is our reserve of strength, the basis upon which it will be possible for us to defeat imperialism and our enemies within this country. A nation which is self-aware, organized and as politically mature as ours can achieve the goals it sets itself.

Debray: There is only one nation, but there are six movements or parties in the Popular Union. Do you see a time in the future when it will be possible to mould them into a single political force?

Allende: Only time can tell. The dynamism of the revolutionary process will progressively create the right conditions for something along the lines of a Revolutionary Party to be formed at some point in time. But to speak now in terms of a single Revolutionary Party is simply Utopian. At some later stage, if conditions continue to progress, it may prove appropriate, but for the time being we have to deal with reality as we find it. This reality is dynamic. The stronger the resistance of our enemies, the stronger our unity will be. And they will go on resisting. I tell you, Régis, they are still plotting; for example, they have set a date on which they are going to act, the 5th of February; we know this and have taken suitable measures, and our response is one they will not forget.

Debray: Besides, a single Party cannot just set itself up by a bureaucratic measure, over the heads of the people.

The most important thing is that the people should need it and express their wish for it.

Allende: Obviously, obviously. Look, Julius Caesar may not have been a Marxist, but he used to say: 'Festina lente.'

Debray: Yes, to go far one has to go at one's own pace. We agree with one another. But I mentioned this because it is a little surprising to find such a multiplicity of movements in the Popular Unity. Surely some, at least, could be combined or merged? Don't you think, for example, that the Catholic Left could be more purposefully united behind the popular programme.

Alende: Of course. There is no lack of political organizations, like the MAPU (Movement of United Popular Action) – a breakaway movement from the Christian Democrats – able to canalize authentic Christian thought, the Christian thought of the left. You have seen it and it is important. The attitude of the Catholic Church in Chile has changed from what it was in the past, and it is an attitude which is lacking in the Church in other parts of the world. Remember the bishops in Medellín and the attitude shown there by the Chilean bishops themselves. You weren't here for the inauguration of the government, but I'll say one thing – the ecumenical Thanksgiving Service was most significant and profound. Moreover, we have here a sector known as the Young Church, a very active sector of militant priests who live in the shanty towns and accompany the settlers when they take over land. Currently, an appeal by the Catholics of the province of Cautín[18] denouncing the estate owners has just been published in the newspapers. There is a very real germ of revolution in those Catholic sectors. We must organize it, we must coordinate it.

Debray: Until now, and currently, the law of the bourgeois has been turned to revolutionary effect, but how long will this procedure work? Until now, bourgeois legality has been turned against the bourgeois themselves. This has been the great strength of the Popular Unity that it has not sacrificed legality to the enemy if one bears in mind the fact that Chile is, so to speak, a country where one calls for a lawyer when there are problems to be solved, whereas in other countries they call for the army. But the time will come when the class enemy will go outside his own laws, and this is already happening. The estate owners in Cautín are armed, and are provoking violent confrontations with the workers on the land. There is a serious amount of arms smuggling from abroad; dangerous subversive plots are being set afoot. How do you intend to cope with sedition?

Allende: To begin with, we are going to contain it with their own laws. Then, we shall meet reactionary violence with revolutionary violence, because we know that they are going to break the rules. For the time being, to stay within the domain of legality, I shall say this. I have already said it. The situation in Chile is such that the Constitution can be changed within the Constitution, by means of plebiscites. There is also another fact, rather paradoxical and difficult to understand. The laws of the people are not the laws of the bourgeoisie. For example, the bourgeoisie made laws which were very lenient to people who occupied land on the grounds that this was not a very serious offence; on the other hand, those who recovered their land received very harsh treatment indeed at the hands of the law. In other words, the law *does not* punish people for occupying land, but it does punish them for recovering it. Why? Because the estate owners were occupying land belonging to the indigenous population, and the native inhabitant who tried to recover his land fell victim to the full force of the law, which protected the estate owner. The bourgeois legislators never for a moment dreamt that their own law would be used against them by the people. What is happening at present? The people occupying the land are the indigenous population, the Mapuche Indians for example, and the people trying to recover it by violent means are the estate owners, who have been dispossessed. Thus, they are feeling the full weight of their own law. Of course, there are limitations: that verdict of the Supreme Court, for example.[19]

Debray: But the Courts are in their hands as well.

Allende: Of course, to a certain extent. And I have to tell you that one of them, the highest, the Supreme Court, has just dealt a blow at the people, and through them, at the Government. The Supreme Court has recently completely cleared a Senator of all inquiries although, in the view of the representatives of the Military Tribunal investigating the assassination of the Commander-in-Chief of the armed forces, he ought to have been interrogated because there are well-founded suspicions about his behaviour. The Ministers of the Court of Appeal were almost unanimous – seventeen out of eighteen – in approving the Military Tribunal's proposal, but it was rejected by a majority of the members of the Supreme Court. This Court, in particular, has been accused of exercizing its duties with a clear class bias. On this occasion, they have prevented the detailed and rigorous investigation of a crime in which reactionary conspirators took part. It is not simply a question of bringing the actual perpetrators of the assassination of the Commander-in-Chief of the Army to book – the people behind the crime, the mind that planned it, must be found.

Debray: Are they going to allow the Schneider case to be thoroughly investigated?

Allende: We are doing everything possible on our side to this purpose, and I believe we shall suceed. Again, don't forget, the Chilean Army's honour and prestige are at stake here. General Schneider was assassinated because he opposed the political conspiracy hatched by the reactionaries. We shall not allow his death to be quietly forgotten. The Commander-in-Chief was the representative of the tradition of the armed forces in Chile. The real culprits of his assassination must be punished.

Debray: And do you believe that those who yesterday defended the oppressors can today defend the oppressed, without themselves changing, without being replaced by others? In other words, can the same Court which yesterday interpreted the Law in favour of the estate-owners interpret it today in favour of the peasants without the

Court itself changing? Can the same police forces who yesterday ejected people from the estates they occupied now turn to the defence of the oppressed?

Allende: We have proposed reforms to the Courts of Law and we shall reform the laws. By implementing Constitutional Reform, we shall bring about changes in the judiciary and, as I have told you, in the event of a proposal for a reform of the Constitutional Charter being totally rejected, we shall resort to the plebiscite, and we shall win, because we shall demonstrate to the people that our modifications are designed to give them justice for the first time. As for the forces responsible for maintaining law and order, you have to agree that it is now us who are enforcing the law. This is what we said during the electoral campaign; the other reactionary political forces carry social disorder within themselves, because they have a vested interest in maintaining a situation which protects a minority by trampling the interests of the majority into the ground. Don't think schematically in terms of the number of votes won by the Popular Unity candidates. Today the Government has much greater support and this will grow still further because the people's awareness will be aroused. I have spoken with the officers of the Corps of Carabineros and told them that we want a police force which is respected by the citizenry, and this because it will be exclusively dedicated to protecting them from delinquency.[20] I told them that they could not use their arms against the people. Shortly after I formed my Government, I called for the resignation of a general in the Carabineros because he had looked on impassively while some estate owners and their employees beat up an official responsible for implementing Land Reform. This official died from the beating he received. The Chief of Carabineros stood by during this incident with two hundred armed men behind him, and did nothing. Of course, had it been a case of peasants attacking landowners, he would have acted violently. This took place before the Popular Unity came into power, but the promotion of this officer who had done nothing to the rank of General was proposed during my Government and it was then that I demanded his resignation. In my opinion he had not done his duty and I made an example of his attitude, and I'm sure that the Corps of Carabineros, at all levels, has understood. The country has understood as well.

Debray: One of the leaders of your party, the Socialist Party, said to me recently: 'If there isn't treason, there's confrontation.' My view is that if there is no confrontation, there will inevitably be treason. Do you think there will be a confrontation?

Allende: Confrontation is already an everyday fact of life, Régis – on all sides, in many different forms.

Debray: I was referring to a head-on decisive confrontation, a violent end to the current state of co-existence. A military uprising for example . . .

Allende: That will depend on them. If they start it, it will happen, but, in any case, we shall wait for them to start it. We are vigilant. But we are not mechanistic. The history of Chile has been punctuated by confrontations for many many years. You must know the long list of massacres of workers and peasants under bourgeois rule. What does one understand by confrontations? As long as there are contradictions in society, and these remain even while we are building socialism, confrontations will occur. Let us leave aside the basic antagonisms: they are settled by the class struggle.

Debray: And the class struggle is going to become keener now.

Allende: Clearly. As you will appreciate, once our constitutional reform is implemented, powerful interests inside and outside the country will suffer. Those people who are going to feel the effect of our Land Reform or the nationalization of the Banks are going to want to react. How could there not be antagonism when our first principles are based on the essential fact of the class struggle? We know that the oligarchical groups, the plutocratic groups, the feudal groups will try to defend their privileges at all costs.

Debray: You refer to 'feudal' sectors and 'oligarchy'.

There could be an element of doubt here, although it is perhaps only a question of terminology. Let me use the occasion to clarify a few concepts. Let us leave to one side the very vexed question of whether estate owners who produce for the home and foreign markets can really be called feudal or semi-feudal and the question of deciding to what extent they are inseparable from and assimilated into capitalist industrial interests proper, and whether these two branches of a dependent economy do not, in the last analysis, form a single class. However, comrade President, I had understood that Chile is not Peru, and that socialist revolution cuts much deeper than military reformism. Or is it a matter of eliminating the backward, inefficient sectors of the bourgeoisie in order to hurl them into a process of modern capitalist development? Or abolishing the archaic agricultural structures in order to modernize the country, in order to offer a bigger home market to the powerful industrial entrepreneurs of the future?

Allende: We use the term 'feudal' sectors in a loose way to indicate what should more accurately be called backward forms of 'Chilean land capitalism'. The backwardness lies in the fact that these capitalist relationships still reveal traces of anachronistic personal fealties, which are steadily dying out, and a great concentration of land ownership, which goes back to a great extent to the property structure of the last century. Again, as is frequent in these cases, there is a large group of small peasants of a quite different type. It is also true that there are very strong ties between a section of these landowners and a section of the urban monopolistic groups. Although it could be claimed in very broad terms that they form a single class, you must admit that there are differences between them as regards the rôle they play in the workings of Chile's dependent capitalism. This has frequently caused major political differences, as in the case of Land Reform. Now, if we take farming, Régis, I don't see the basis of your anxiety if the problem is analysed in the context of the overall changes proposed in our programme. As you know, for many years now, Land Reform, taken in isolation, is well known as one of the so-called democratic bourgeois changes, in other words a change which can act as a stimulant to capitalism itself. However, in the modern world, when the fundamental conflict has reached the stage of socialist transformations, it is accepted that a far-reaching Land Reform, corresponding to the interests of the agricultural labourers and the various categories of medium-size and small peasants, can only be carried out through an alliance of all the oppressed classes, headed by the working class. In our case, Land Reform is not accompanied by the maintenance of capitalism, but by the destruction of its fundamental nucleus: national and foreign monopolistic capitalism. It is not, therefore, a case of developing capitalism in the countryside, but a process of guiding tenurial structures towards Socialism by the means which are best suited to the character of our historical and social development. It is understood that, in some cases, the new structure will be of the most advanced type – communal ownership; elsewhere various forms of cooperative system; and finally, the survival of sectors of small private ownership will have to be considered.

Debray: One might say, then, Comrade President, that you are carrying out your political programme, and that, as a result, the state of confrontation is continuous?

Allende: Yes, a permanent state. If they bring it on themselves, if they provoke it, there will be a constant state of confrontation, and we're ready for it psychologically. Have no doubt of it.

Debray: I don't doubt it. But it isn't a question of you and the Government being ready – the people must also be able to resist; they must be aware that here, perhaps tomorrow, they could find themselves in extreme situations.

Allende: We have told them this, repeatedly; the people know this. Moreover, as I have already told you, our struggle goes back many years; there is a great degree of awareness, this is no surprise to the people. What we have to do is to give them a few examples, like the Supreme

Court decision. As President and head of one State body, I am obliged under the present administrative system to respect the decisions of the other State body, but this by no means prevents me reflecting on the implications, the political repercussions of such a system, particularly in the case of a decision which, in my view, restricts the possibility of making a full investigation into the death of General Schneider, which is, in effect, the investigation into a right-wing conspiracy. This is my duty: to tell the people, to tell them to be more watchful, and this is what I shall do.

Debray: Are many people involved in the assassination of General Schneider?

Allende: Any number of them. There's a whole group of people who represented, and still represent, believe me, the interests of high finance and the political interests of the reactionary Right.

Debray: Are they from within Chile only?

Allende: From inside and outside.

II

Debray: Comrade President, something caught my attention in the speech you made in Valparaiso yesterday. Speaking to that great mass of people, you said: 'I shall not make critical references to the Supreme Court. They are there, we are here.' What did you mean by that, because I didn't understand too well?

Allende: Well now, in the programme of the Popular Unity, we explained that we want a genuinely independent Judiciary, a Judiciary whose senior members are drawn from the single house of Government. What is more, the parties, especially the Socialist Party, have criticized the decisions of the Supreme Court and certain eminent lawyers, among them Eduardo Novoa,[21] the President of the Fiscal Defence Council, have confirmed that the Supreme Court is showing an ever-increasing tendency to give a high, very high, percentage of decisions in favour of the privileged classes. To state matters plainly, I must repeat that what they are practising is class justice.

Debray: In other words, the workers are perhaps in power, but they certainly have no power in the judiciary.

Allende: Precisely.

Debray: Aren't you worried by these restrictions?

Allende: Yes, very worried. But as we have said, I shall respect the limitations imposed by a system which is not of our making while the three powers exist independently, and it was with some irony that I said that I am not going to criticize. But you are aware that in fact I have criticized and explained the political implications of their findings, stating my view that the fact that that senator was allowed to go scot free practically rendered it impossible to investigate the principal suspects, and I added that I would use all means – judicial, legal and administrative – at my disposal to find the real culprits.

Debray: There is something else which has struck me, comrade President, a phrase you repeat fairly frequently: 'We are a canal, not a dam.' But I have the impression that, in spite of everything, you have been something of a dam in the containment of land seizures, the movements of squatters and the encampments of the homeless. Not a dam of the type constituted by the Frei government, it goes without saying, because the Christian Democrats ordered the Carabineros, and the Mobile Guard which has been disbanded by the Popular Unity, to use force to eject the homeless, the landless peasants who invaded property. The massacres at the estates of 'San Miguel' and Puerto Montt[22] are ample evidence of this. Clearly, a Popular Government cannot act like that, but on the other hand, you are not encouraging the dispossessed to act.

Allende: On 4 September, one stage in the historic process in which the nation is engaged was completed, and on 3 November we achieved another step when we formed our Government. For this reason, we lose no opportunity in asking our comrades to understand that they should therefore have confidence in what we are doing and in what we are going to do. The problem is a clear one, Régis. I know of no country which has wholly solved its housing problem. Including Cuba. Indeed, I disagree with many aspects of their urban reform, because I don't believe that they are the right answer, and I've said so to Fidel. We want to face up to the housing problem squarely. We want to provide housing, but we are not in favour of any anarchical approaches to the solution of the problem. In Chile today, there are thousands and thousands of shanty-town dwellers who do not have drinking water in their homes, and the women, in particular, have to go out to wherever there is a water tap and fill their pitchers. If we allow the cities to go on spreading outwards with makeshift single-storey dwellings, it will be impossible to provide drinking water, draining, electricity, gas, light, etc., for every house. Imagine the cost of providing each household with all these amenities. There are areas where we cannot build isolated single-storey houses; we shall have to build blocks of flats because it is convenient to use the advantages of height.

Debray: And are the people attached to individual houses?

Allende: They're attached to the idea of the 'individualistic house'.

Debray: Perhaps this, as an ideal pattern of a particular way of life, is symptomatic of the way a certain bourgeois ideology is influencing things.

Allende: And this must be overcome, and the only way to do this is by using arguments that people understand, and are aware of. You understand this perfectly well, it's the same as what happened with the land seizures, isn't it? There is a law, and without doubt that law is going to be the instrument with which we shall expropriate the estates, all properties exceeding the minimum established by the law, namely 80 hectares of irrigated land in the central region. But what we are concerned to do is to carry out Land Reform on a regional basis to ensure that the production which Chile needs is kept up, and the climate, soil and region are taken into account in determining the pattern of this production. If this is done in an anarchical way, it would be impossible to plan production. This is the problem, and this is why the people must understand that we are not a dam, but a canal. The people can never be a dam if the people are the Government. It is worse still for workers to seize houses which are completed or under construction when these houses belong to other workers. We cannot accept confrontation between members of the same class. That is anarchy.

Debray: Returning to the theme of class confrontation, and if I may give you my personal view, I rather doubt that the Right would be stupid enough to provoke an immediate break. Do you not think that there is more to fear from the silent protest of the bourgeoisie? Do you not think that they are waging a kind of trench war, a subtle, stubborn war of attrition, rather than a war of movement.

Allende: We must be on our guard against both. They're using both, Régis: the trench war and the war of movement.

Debray: They would seem to have lost the war of movement up to the present. But the trench war continues on all fronts, not only in the immediate sphere of the political struggle. There are many means of infiltration or containment by which a Popular Government and its revolutionary process can be restricted or side-tracked into bourgeois formats. You know what they are: it might be an excessive respect for legality, or opportunism, the rat-race for public offices, bureaucratization, or the depoliticization of the masses, who would thus be exposed to the ideology of the exploiting class, that is of the bourgeoisie. It could be a lot of things. Perhaps the greatest danger, because it is less easy to discern, is this: a progressive takeover from within by the class adversary. How do you see the problem, comrade President?

Allende: I'll tell you, comrade Debray. I believe they have two possibilities: one is the one you've just described, which we could call the trench war. Up to the present, they've lost the other war, the war of movement, but this does not mean they've cried off. They need to marshal their forces. If they could have, they would have done it.

Debray: So they resort to other approaches, other methods?

Allende: The approach you have indicated.

Debray: Which is not only found in Chile, as you know, it can be found in certain Socialist countries . . .

Allende: And more advanced ones. The only answer to this is a large-scale campaign to instill consciousness: the constant awareness of the masses, direct participation in problems, a vigilant attitude and awareness among the militants in the Parties. This is undoubtedly a factor which is going to lend dynamism to the process; at the same time either subversive or open resistance welds the Popular Unity more firmly and thus stems the opposition. Because we are in a struggle, we have an adversary, we have our enemy and if we discern attitudes in certain forms, it is logical that we should act, that we should take steps, that we should intensify our activity. You have seen that we are striking daily – nobody imagined that we would be so quick to enter into diplomatic relations with China, did they? Nor did they believe that we would establish trading relations with Vietnam and Korea, but we have.

Debray: And perhaps in this respect, the transfer of the seat of Government to a provincial capital, Valparaiso, has something to do with this struggle against bureaucratic red tape.

Allende: Yes of course, because in the provinces more than elsewhere, one feels the slowness of progress, the lack of effective action, the absence of achievements, things we have become familiar with under previous governments. We must break with all this, and this is why I said yesterday that the Popular Government must change in both form and substance. Here, we are going to study the fundamental problems with the community, it is here that we are going to square up to the solutions and make the people participate and make them take an active part in the important discussions. We want the workers, the peasants, the intellectuals and the students all to play their part.

Debray: In connection with this idea of participation, you said often that power is born from the grassroots. Will the political parties making up the Popular Unity be enough? Do you not think that the CUP (Popular Unity Committees) in their present form could be revitalized, could be given a different content so that the people could gain increasing control over their living conditions, beginning by controlling the prices and quality of consumer goods, and rising gradually to their involvement in the defence of the Revolution?

Allende: We must organize the masses, we must organize the homeless, the unemployed, we must organize our women to watch food prices and quality. For example, Régis, as I said yesterday, the National Women's Movement now has 20,000 members, and they are going to do voluntary welfare work; together, they will contribute 160,000 hours of voluntary work a month and that is really something. This is active participation; they will be helping in the distribution of milk, combating the refuse problem, instructing mothers in how to avoid diarrhoea in infants, and, on the subject we were discussing a moment ago, monitoring the price and quality of, for example, bread.

Debray: Has it been possible to freeze prices, broadly speaking?

Allende: Completely, up to now.

Debray: In one of your speeches, I read this: 'We are not now going to have any grand duke of the Public Administration', and you also said something which I didn't understand very well: 'We shall not allow any workers' aristocracy.' What were you referring to? Perhaps to something which was very surprising to people outside the country: the fact that the miners in Chuquicamata voted for the Right. This is difficult to understand. The working class voted for Allende, but in a few areas . . .

Allende: Very few . . .

Debray: Very few . . . they voted for Alessandri in areas where there were imperialist companies.

Allende: No, only in Chuqui; not in El Salvador, nor in

El Teniente. More significantly, in one ward in El Salvador all 300 registered voters went to the poll and I got 300 votes; in other words, 100% of those workers supported the candidate of the Popular Unity.

Debray: This was to be expected – what was abnormal was what happened in Chuquicamata.[23] How do you explain that?

Allende: Look, it's explained like this: as you well know, the trade union organizations have established certain areas of power and influence within the framework of our bourgeois democratic regime. The life of the copper workers is hard, a high proportion of them suffer from occupational diseases like silicosis, but this hardship is compensated for by the high wages which the foreign companies mining copper in Chile are able to pay them since they are making such high profits out of the nation's natural resources. For years, the North American companies have been telling them that the day they leave Chile, the workers, particularly those earning dollars, would be much worse off. We have only meagre means of communication with which to break down the frame of mind imposed by the dominant class on a section of the population which lives largely in isolation. You should remember that Chuquicamata is practically an isolated citadel dominated by imperialist business interests. We must struggle to bring the truth home to these workers – it is not enough that they should have trade union organization, until and unless it is steeped in revolutionary ideology. The Communist and Socialist Parties have struggled to uphold the revolutionary ideology of the 'Central Unica de Trabajadores' (Single Workers' Union). We are also trying to get the people to organize themselves. I should tell you that only 20% of the working class in Chile is organized, and therefore 80%, the vast majority, are not organized.

Debray: And how do you explain this deficiency?

Allende. There are many reasons: firstly, past Governments have not made it easy for the workers to organize, because they were class-biased Governments. You know that an organized worker is a much more powerful worker, more aware and in a better position to fight for his rights.

Debray: And they didn't grant legal status to the Single Workers' Union (CUT)?

Allende: No, but we shall be able to.

Debray: You intend to promote the trade union movement, to place it on a broader footing?

Allende: We want it to be universal. Open to all workers, including those in the public sector. They have an organization, but it isn't recognized. However, the public sector is different; for example, I've read that, in France, even the police have threatened to go on strike. In Chile, in the context of our bourgeois democratic outlook, this would be unacceptable to the Chileans. We are going to provide our civil servants with an authentic organization as well, but on the basis of their understanding that this is their Government and that it is not necessary for them to strike in order to solve their problems. What actually happens? The copper workers, for example, were and are aware that a strike in the copper industry lasting sixty or thirty days is a strike which no Government can tolerate, because this would be a terrible blow to Chile, and it would represent a great loss of revenue to the State. Therefore, logically, they have the powerful lever of knowing that any strike by them affects the national economy, and any Government is obliged to solve the problem. And how do they solve it. Well, by giving them a large part of what they demand. So what's the answer? The workers in the copper industry must understand that they are not going to enjoy a privileged position far above that of other workers simply because they are in the copper industry. Their class status must remain the same, they must realize that we need their work and their productivity for Chile, and that the vast majority of them have a living wage. These are the facts, this is the heart of the matter, it's a problem of conscience, a question of class consciousness on the part of the people. In the copper industry, a proportion of the workers are promoted to staff positions, and a percentage of the staff, even if they are Chilean, are paid in dollars. Some of these, I'm not saying all, used to sell their dollars on the black market and so when you asked them how much they earn, they told you the equivalent in escudos at black market prices, rather than at the official exchange rate.

Debray: With regard to the rôle of the workers in the centres of production, you have indicated that in the area of social economy, the Government was going to give a share in the management of companies to the workers.

Allende: And to the white collar workers and technical personnel as well.

Debray: For me, since you are a Socialist and since I am aware of the long-standing if remote relations between the Socialist Party and Yugoslavia, this brings worker's control to mind.

Allende: No, no. We have insisted on the participation of manual and white collar workers and technical personnel in the management of our enterprises, but this does not mean that these enterprises are going to enjoy independence as regards their production. We are and always shall be in favour of a centralized economy, and companies will have to conform to the Government's production planning. To achieve this, we shall maintain a continuous dialogue with the workers. But we are not going to hand over a company to the workers just so that they can produce what they want or to let them turn the fact that they control a company which is of vital importance to their country to their own personal advantage in order to demand higher earnings than other people. We are against any policy of that nature.

Debray: So you are aiming at democratic planning along the lines of controlled planning, but with the workers having a share in decisions.

Allende: Of course, otherwise it would be impossible to achieve the development we need. This is why we said to the workers – to take a case in point, my visit to the coal mines (I very much regret not having asked you to come with me; I really wish I had done because you would have seen the area and talked with the workers) – well, now, what did I say to the workers? This: you are now producing 3,800 tons of coal a day; we need to produce 4,700, so we need to increase productivity, you have to work harder, produce more, sacrifice more. But they are not going to sacrifice themselves to fill the coffers of the private company for which they work. Now they are going to work for themselves: we're going to give them better conditions, we're going to give them housing suitable for human beings, we're going to give them sports grounds, we're going to give them milk for their children, we're going to give them educational facilities, and they are going to work for the country. We still need coal as a source of energy, the more so since our oil resources are running down. This is the importance of the workers being aware of national problems, and of their realizing that whether they work in the coal mines, or in the copper mines, or on the land, their work is for Chile and not merely centred around their own personal problems or problems within their own trades.

Debray: Giving them an awareness of power, in other words.

Allende: Exactly, and also of what this power represents for the country and for our national economic development plans.

Debray: That is to say free from small-minded attitudes, free from regionalism, free from self-interest. We could look a little more closely at the relationship between the working class, as a class enjoying hegemony or not, and political power. You are well aware that it is one thing to be in a position of political dominance and another to be able to exercise the social, moral and cultural leadership of a given society. Even when the workers hold political power it is possible for the bourgeoisie to continue imposing its ideology, controlling cultural standards and social behaviour patterns. Without talking of the powers of survival of the institutional apparatus which impedes the direct expression of the initiative of the masses, what could cause anxiety is the survival of that widespread control which a dominant class can still retain even when the banks and monopolistic companies have been nationalized. Clearly, these are not the problems of the day, but what is a problem in the immediate term is the question of the mass communication media. Today, as in the past, these are controlled by money, not by the people. I imagine that for you as a ruler, this is a difficult problem.

Allende: It certainly is. And we are aware of the problem.

Debray: Do you intend to solve it in any way?

Allende: Yes, as we have said, we are not going to suppress the communications media which are in bourgeois hands, but we are going to coordinate our own, we are going to increase them, and we are going to ensure that those who work in these media, the journalists, clearly understand that they will be the first to benefit by change, so that even when they are working in bourgeois companies and they see that their employers' policy is against the Popular Government, they are, by their presence in these companies, an element of resistance against the bourgeoisie. You see, when the journalist feels secure and knows that he can find work elsewhere, he can say to the company: 'Look, I'm not publishing this information', or: 'I'm going to print the facts.' For example, Régis, you were at the meeting in Valparaiso yesterday – well now, for the first time in the history of Chile (and you know that I have been a candidate for many years, many times; I've been a presidential candidate for eighteen years) but for the first time in the history of Chile, *El Mercurio* published an authentic photograph showing the crowds attending a mass meeting.

Debray: The first time?

Allende: The first time. Had the meeting been held before the elections, they would have said 3,000 people, and in fact they said 40,000, and this was the correct figure.

Debray: But didn't you hold meetings attended by even greater crowds when you were a candidate?

Allende: Yes, but what did they say? That there had been a meeting of a few thousand people, full stop.

That 3,000 or 5,000 Allende supporters gathered to acclaim him in Talca, Valparaiso or Concepción. In fact, there were mass meetings of one hundred thousand or three hundred thousand people, but they never made any reference to the actual numbers.

Debray: But in addition to the meetings you hold – and I don't want to criticize you of course, because I am here as your guest – but I'll put this to you in the form of a question.

Allende: You have every right to criticize – that's what dialogue is all about.

Debray: I'll put it as a question nevertheless: there are three television channels here; why do you not address the people in some manner which is less rigid, less formal than that required when you are announcing decrees? Why don't you address the people more often to explain what you are doing, to discuss it with the press and representatives of the people. Why don't you allow yourself to be seen by the whole country chatting informally in the way we are doing now?

Allende: For two reasons: the first of which is that previous Governments exploited what we call the compulsory national radio and television channels to such excess that finally the people became bored by it all and rejected such programmes. The other reason is that I do not want my Government to become a one-man show by the comrade President. This is why I have instructed my Ministers and senior civil servants to take part in television discussion programmes to explain the problems with which their ministries are concerned. You've got to remember that, of the three television channels, only one is controlled by the State; what's more, the Television Authority imposes fairly strict limitations on the Government – this has been a manoeuvre of a political nature. The other two channels belong to the Universities. These are facts which have a bearing on the issue and have to be taken into consideration. At all events, I think one or two Ministers take part in television discussion programmes each week, and I believe that I myself, without setting myself any preconceived plan, have made appearances every ten days or so. I have decided to concentrate on doing this for important issues.

Debray: A parallel question. In the actions, speeches and limited discreet propaganda of the Popular Unity, there is a recurring theme: 'the new man', 'the new ethic', etc... Doesn't it seem Utopian to you to talk in these terms when you have a society which is still so essentially bourgeois, in which the old educational structures have yet to be removed?

Allende: No. We are fully aware that the educated people brought up in this society have nothing in common with what we call 'the new man'. Bourgeois ideology is dominant in our society as it stands, but it is quite clear that what we call 'the new man' will emerge to become the citizen of the new society. Our task now is to make a major effort in the field of education in order to awake interest in forming a new society in the consciousness of the masses, and presenting the image of the members of this new society, 'the new men'. Now the vanguard contains revolutionaries who are determined to behave as such, and it is clear that they are laying the foundations from which 'the new man' will emerge. I do not, therefore, consider it Utopian to talk in these terms, although it would indeed be if we were to imagine that this man was going to live in our society as it is at the moment. The 'new man' is going to emerge in the new society.

Debray: The economic foundations of which remain to be built...

Allende: They will have been established when 'the new man' has been fashioned by the new social co-existence, when we have a classless society, when we have a socialist society.

Debray: In other words, these are not the problems of the moment, are they? But let us speak of the problems of the moment. The nationalizations have been very far-reaching, affecting copper, coal and other key industries, but what I have not understood is the policy of compensation which the Popular Government intends to follow.

It has been said that the payment of these amounts of compensation to the foreign companies is a high price to pay for maintaining social peace and even, perhaps, for keeping Chile at peace. What is your view of this problem? Won't this be impoverishing the State to the advantage of the monopolies?

Allende: Firstly, there is no commitment to compensation in the case of copper. We shall study the situation in each industry; initial capital investment, earnings, excess profits in relation to the market, depreciation, etc., and we can pay anything between not one peso and a billion dollars. This is our problem; what we do not want, and we have said so openly, is that it should be said that we are going to usurp and misappropriate what is not ours to take. Take the example of the option we have offered to the holders of shares in banks; this was done mainly to avoid hurting the small shareholders. We cannot lay ourselves open on all fronts; that would be stupid and unjust. On the other hand, by spending a few millions here, we are saving on the cost of what resistance, confrontation or a possible arms race might otherwise have involved us in.

Debray: On the subject of arms, I understand the revolutionaries here are not too well supplied, not even well enough for self-defence. I've seen an article on Chile in a French left-wing magazine which carried the headline: THE REVOLUTION WITHOUT GUNS. Does this formula seem realistic to you? Of course, there has been no use, or very little use, of guns here in Chile, but is what is happening here really a revolution?

Allende: I believe so. We are at a revolutionary stage. Tell me, how do you define a revolution? From the sociological point of view?

Debray: I would like to clear up one point straight away. For me, the question of violence is not a vital issue.

Allende: Good. It is the transfer of power from a minority class to a majority class.

Debray: It is indeed – at least as a bare definition.

Allende: Here the minority class has been ousted by the people, and this has been demonstrated, because if the

minority class were in power, there would be no nationalization of copper, no nationalization of the banks and no
land reform, Régis.

Debray: But to date, the Government has not, shall we
say, stepped outside the reformist framework. It has acted
within the Constitution it inherited from the previous,
bourgeois, Government; it has acted within the established
institutional framework, and it can therefore be said that
what there has been to date is reform. It was in about
1905, I believe, that Lenin made the distinction between
two types of reform, that which is destined to open the
road to socialist revolution, and that which is destined to
side-track it, and finally obstruct it.

Allende: I believe that we have used those which open
the road to revolution. We make the claim, and I say this
in all modesty, that we are creating a different way and
demonstrating that it is possible to make the fundamental
changes on which the road to revolution is built. We have
said that we are going to create a democratic, national,
revolutionary and popular Government which will open
the road to socialism because socialism cannot be imposed
by decree. All the measures we have adopted are measures
which lead to the revolution.

Debray: But there was a certain historical background
to my question. There has been a Popular Front here,
there have been democratic governments. You yourself
were a Minister under Pedro Aguirre Cerda. Then
González Videla's Government,[24] which ended badly, when
the Cold War started; then Ibañez's populism. That was a
failure, not only here, but throughout the Continent.

Allende: What was a failure? I beg your pardon.

Debray: A certain collaborationist, conciliatory policy
based on a simple electoral combination between workers'
parties and what one might call bourgeois democratic
parties. That was a failure. How can you, comrade
President, be sure that the failures of the past will not be
repeated in Chile in 1970.

Allende: Firstly, Régis, I maintain that the Chilean
Popular Front was not a failure, for one very simple

reason: the Chilean Popular Front did not set out to bring about the revolutionary transformation of Chile. Pedro Aguirre Cerda drew up a programme whose catchword was: 'Food, housing and clothing'. That is, it was a humanitarian programme, but not one of social content, still less revolutionary. Anyone who thinks Pedro Aguirre Cerda was a revolutionary would, of course, have to say that he failed. But the fact is that we consciously entered into a coalition in order to form the left wing of the system – the capitalist system, that is. By contrast, today, as our programme shows, we are struggling to change the system, and this is completely different. In the Popular Front, Régis, there was a dominant Party, a majority party, the party of the bourgeoisie, the Radical Party. Today, there is no dominant party in the Popular Unity, but there are two parties of the working class, revolutionary parties, Marxist parties. Finally, comrade, the President of the Republic is a socialist. Things are different, then, and I have reached this office in order to bring about the economic and social transformation of Chile, to open up the road to socialism. Our objective is total, scientific, Marxist socialism.

Debray: Also, the international context is different.

Allende: Of course. When will we get there? Well, I was in China in '53. How old was the revolution in China then?

Debray: Three or four years.

Allende: A little more I think.

Debray: Didn't Mao enter Peking in January 1949?

Allende: All right. What was happening in Shanghai, for example? There were still semi-private companies. There was still Hong Kong. The English still had customs advantages in Shanghai. Everyone knows that China, the People's Republic, could finish off Formosa in twenty-four hours. Why don't they do it? Simply because this would be jeopardizing world peace and their own revolution. Why doesn't Fidel take Guantánamo? Is anyone going to say that Fidel wouldn't like to be rid of the Americans there? Why doesn't he take it?

Debray: But I would like to make clear that I am not, of course, an advocate of measures of this nature. It is not my wish to be cast in the rôle of ultra-leftist all the time! I believe you are absolutely right to take your time, to do things at your own speed. The main question calling for discrimination is not the issue of the use of one form or another of physical violence; the main question is: which sector of society is the motive force behind the process, which class is in charge of the administration of the process?

Allende: The proletariat; that is, the working class.

Debray: If this is so, and this situation is maintained and consolidated, then there would be guarantees. Not to mention the constitutional guarantees . . .

Allende: . . . which we had to give, because this meant we could take up government without compromising our programme in any way.

Debray: Was it absolutely necessary? Was it essential to negotiate that Statute on democratic guarantees?[25]

Allende: Yes, that's why we did it. I am still convinced that it was right to introduce the guarantees Statute, but I should make it clear that the use of the word negotiation is unjustified here, because we did not give ground on a single line of our Government programme. Put yourself in the period in which this Statute got onto the books, and you will see it as a tactical necessity. We have spoken at some length about the dramatic period between 4 September and 24 October. Think of a Chile under the scourge of the so-called 'Terror Campaign', the name given to the war of psychological intimidation waged against the people by their enemies. This campaign was conducted at a time when the outside world was looking on in amazement at this little country and saying: 'For the first time a Marxist has reached power by winning an election.' A sector of the Christian Democrat Party, headed by one of its leaders, Radomiro Tomic, came to the conclusion that if their Party did not contribute its Senators' and Deputies' votes towards the establishment of a majority which would make our victory viable, there would be civil war in Chile. This sector therefore proposed that the victory of the Popular Unity be recognized in exchange for a 'Statute of Guarantees'. Whereas they said that we inspire terror, tinged as we are with the ideology of the revolutionary class, they admitted at the same time that they couldn't be responsible for civil war. Hence the 'Statute' was born. Read it and compare it with our Government programme, and you will come to the conclusion that we did not change one comma of our programme. At the time, the important thing was to take control of the Government.

Debray: Shall we look back at something else. Given the circumstances; since the programme of the Popular Unity was known from before the elections, and since your personality, and particularly your recent political career, were also well known, how do you explain that the bourgeoisie, well, the Right, the other side shall we say, split its vote by putting up two candidates? I know the question is a little specious, since Tomic's programme bears many similarities to your own, but how do you explain the disunity of the Right in the face of a left wing whose objectives were so clearly defined?

Allende: We touched on this during our talk in Santiago. I said that many factors were involved, and that one of these factors certainly cannot be compared to experience in other countries. The fact is that the Right in Chile firstly did not believe that the Christian Democrats could win because of the errors they had committed, because of their lack of decisive impact, and because they wouldn't get the vote of the hard core traditional right, and still less that of the left. So they pinned their hopes on a name – because if Jorge Alessandri hadn't existed, the Right would not have found a candidate they could build into a myth; they believed in the myth, and Alessandri was also very much in favour of the general dissemination of this belief. For them, the image of Alessandri was the complete answer, it crossed all political boundaries, it was an ineffable light. Alessandri would win because he was Alessandri. There is something you must appreciate: in this country, history has shown that individuals, names, have an enormous influence. Alessandri's father filled fifty years of Chile's history; Ibañez, forty. Hence the choice of Jorge Alessandri, who had been President, and had been active in politics since the time of his father – a participation of some forty years or more in the history of our country. And, modesty apart, I too, although a comparative newcomer, have played my part in the history of Chile for thirty years.

Debray: Didn't they expect the popular success?

Allende: Ah no, never.

Debray: Perhaps a new law – or anti-law – of history will have to be invented: the law of surprises. Whenever anything important happens in history, it is always by surprise.

Allende: No, not exactly by surprise. The general situation is influenced by a particular set of temporal circumstances.

Debray: And the surprise factor played an important part here.

Allende: But let me tell you something. It is incredible that the Right should have allowed circumstances to play such a part, because they had the experience of '64 to call on. They knew that if there had been three candidates, I would have been President in '64 and the proof of this is that they withdrew their support of the candidate of the Right of the day and supported Frei.

Debray: What would you call this? Blindness?

Allende: Pride. In the case of the Right, insolence. And, in general, an inadequate understanding of the interplay of opposition between sectors of society.

Debray: Yes. Perhaps another factor is a widespread social upheaval in Latin America, an awakening of anti-imperialist awareness, a new awareness of the political bankruptcy of the capitalist system in the dependent countries which is even to be found in many sectors of the bourgeoisie itself. I believe that Tomic could be described as a product of this radicalization of the petty bourgeoisie.

Allende: Exactly, nobody can dispute this. There

were many respects in which Tomic's programme had very much in common with our own, and some would say that it was even more advanced than ours on some points.[26]

Debray: Comrade President, allow me to look ahead a little. You know that Leninism has nothing against compromise, as long as tactical compromises serve as a useful purpose in the revolutionary strategy of the proletariat, as long as they are absolutely necessary and do not jeopardize the long-term development of the class struggle. The conciliatory conditions under which the process we are seeing today is progressing doubtless correspond to the objective and specific conditions of Chile. The problem now is whether these conditions can continue to favour the advancement of this process; in other words, how can the transition from a bourgeois system to another more democratic, more revolutionary, more proletarian system be achieved without a break? History contains many examples of a social class which, to avoid being overthrown prefers to sacrifice a finger or two to save the hand and the arm. One may wonder whether the proletariat and their allies are going to be hemmed in by the bourgeois institutions, and pacified with a few reforms here and there, or whether at a given moment the framework will be broken to create a proletarian democracy? Is the proletariat going to assert itself over the bourgeoisie, or will the bourgeoisie gradually remould the proletariat and re-absorb it into its world. Doubtless, I'm over-generalizing, but basically my question would be: 'Who is using who? Who is taking who for a ride?' That's putting it brutally and perhaps a little provocative . . .

Allende: I don't believe that a comrade can ask me questions whose intention is to provoke.

Debray: Well, there are those who say I'm a professional 'agent provocateur', comrade President.

Allende: I shall not allow myself to be provoked.

Debray: The question is important.

Allende: And the answer is short: the proletariat.

Debray: This is a gamble at this stage, because as you

know and as you have explained, Popular Fronts are no longer viable and can never be repeated.

Allende: No, this is not a Popular Front, that has to be made quite clear.

Debray: What should one call it then, a Workers' Front,

Allende: A Workers' Front, a Patriotic Front, a Popular Unity, but with a backbone, in which the working class is indisputably the driving force, because although we do not have the hegemony of a single party, the Socialist and Communist Parties are undoubtedly the parties which represent ninety per cent of the workers – workmen, peasants, office workers, technicians and professional people. Well now, the question is: 'Who is going to use who?' Even accepting the form of the question, the answer is the proletariat. If it wasn't so, I wouldn't be here. I am working for Socialism and through Socialism.

Debray: Your answer convinces me. The more so since what is happening in Chile today is taking place against a particular international background and the balance of power in the world has changed a lot since the years of the pre-war Popular Front. One has to bear this very strongly in mind since outside this country, many people are saying things like: 'Chile is the England of Latin America' and 'they are a good people, they are like us, not tropical, they don't like violence', etc... But my understanding of the situation is that what is happening in Chile is squarely in line with the worldwide struggle against imperialism. Is this true or not?

Allende: Yes.

Debray: Did you take part in the Tri-Continental Conference in Havana?

Allende: I was Chairman of the Chilean delegation, and it was I who proposed the OLAS.[27]

Debray: And you presumably haven't altered any of your views since then?

Allende: No.

Debray: Is popular Chile still in the Tri-Continental?

Allende: I'm sorry?

Debray: I don't mean within the Tri-Continental

organization, but, as we were discussing a moment ago, taking part in the anti-imperialist struggle which is being fought in the three Continents, without, of course, prejudicing the proletarian anti-capitalist struggle in the metropolitan countries.

Allende: Sorry, I want to be clear on this, especially with a comrade like yourself. A group or delegation representing the Socialist and Communist Parties went to the Tri-Continental Conference. We took part in the Conference, Socialists and Communists together, and I proposed the creation of OLAS because there were such organizations in Africa and Asia and I considered that there should be a regional organization in Latin America which would be the third leg of the tripod so that there could be one in Asia, one in Africa and a third in Latin America. Now, since I proposed this, I have always maintained that OLAS could not be the supranational revolutionary headquarters.

Debray: Evidently. This would be taking an idealistic view of a very complex process which cannot be handled like a military operation, with a general staff moving flags around a map.

Allende: Exactly, I have always maintained that OLAS had to be an information organization, a unit for coordination and demonstration of solidarity. And this is so much so that in my capacity as President of the Senate, I said roundly and categorically that I was not the President of OLAS, but I was a member of the Directorate of OLAS and would not renounce this position even if they censured me for it, but they didn't dare to do so. In fact, the Christian Democrats had no right to censure me because they have an international organization. So my answer to your question is this: the Chilean Government is not in OLAS. Why? Because there are parties in the Chilean Government like the Radical Party which was not in OLAS and the MAPU Party which was not in OLAS, but the Communists and the Socialists are still in OLAS. However, quite frankly, OLAS has never been very strong here.

Debray: No, OLAS has been, shall we say, a stepping stone. But what is perhaps surprising is that the Chilean Government should remain in the Organization of American States, that same OAS which was described recently by Fidel as a brothel. Chile then, is a frequenter of this brothel. It is all the more difficult to understand because it was stated in the programme of the Popular Unity – as everybody knows since it was announced before the election – that they would denounce the present OAS and that the Popular Government would work towards the creation of an Organization which was truly representative of the countries of Latin America. Is the contradiction apparent or real?

Allende: Look, Régis. I helped draw up that programme, but without doubt, if you look at the context of Latin America, you will see, won't you, that the majority of Governments – and I don't want to be too categorical because I am President of Chile – you will appreciate that it is very difficult to create any body which is truly representative of the Latin American peoples without the United States being represented in some way. Under these circumstances, therefore, I believe that it would be a gross error to give up this platform. Moreover, the case of Cuba is different, because the Cubans were thrown out of OAS.

Debray: But they say they will never return.

Allende: Of course. Why? Because Fidel Castro and Cuba have suffered the consequences of imperialist policy. Cuba left the OAS when another phase of the plan to isolate it and break it economically succeeded, namely the decision, which Chile did not vote in favour of, to expel it from the OAS. The United States' economic blockade of Cuba was carried out without the agreement of the OAS on the initiative of the American State Department, and I can therefore understand Fidel's assessment of the OAS. Now, we are well aware of our limitations, but I say that for us it is necessary, it is absolutely essential that we use this platform to make our points of view heard and to explain the changes which need to be made in the OAS.

Debray: And in this way perhaps it will be able to play

a positive rôle as things change, and things change rapidly in this continent. Now then, as to your relations with the United States; do you have reason to believe they will get worse? What do you expect?

Allende: If we look at history, we certainly have plenty to fear. Latin America's experience in this respect is dramatic and bloody. We could talk about the strong-arm politics, or dollar politics, or sending in marines. We are familiar with all this, but at the same time we feel that the United States as a people and as a nation is today going through times which are very different from those of the past. They have deep-seated internal problems. Not just the race question, but problems with certain sectors of the working population, with the students and with the intellectuals who do not accept the policy of aggression. Also, they have provoked world-wide repulsion by their attitude in Vietnam, and it is therefore more difficult for them to operate in Latin America. There is no aggression in our attitude to the North American people.

Debray: And the aggression would come from them, if it were to come at all?

Allende: I will say this: from our side, there will not even be verbal aggression. Mr Nixon is President of the United States and I am President of Chile. I shall have nothing derogatory to say about Mr Nixon as long as Mr Nixon respects the President of Chile. If they break with their obligation, if once again they cast aside the priniciples of self-determination and non-intervention, they will meet with a reply worthy of a people and its representative.

Debray: They know this, and I don't think they will do anything stupid, but there are other forms of aggression: economic measures, blockades.

Allende: I believe that they will not do anything of this nature; firstly, because as I say, we have acted within the laws of Chile, within the Constitution. It is for this reason, Régis, that I have maintained that victory through the polling booths was the way to pre-empt any such policy, because this way their hands are tied.

Debray: It means that any intervention would have no

legitimate justification. But when it's a question of intervening, the truth is that they have scant respect for international law. Finally, in your view, what is the lesson to be
drawn from what is happening in Chile? What, would
you say, is the lesson for Latin America?

Allende: The lesson is that each country has its own
particular circumstances, and it is in the light of these
circumstances that one must act. There is no set formula.
Our case, for example, opens up possibilities, it shows
a way. We have arrived through the polling booths.
Apparently it can be said of us that we are mere reformers,
but we have taken measures which imply that we want to
bring about the revolution, that is transform society, and
that in turn means build the socialist society.

Debray: You know how in the overall picture of Latin
America your image is being used as a counter-balance to
those of Fidel and Ché. What do you think of those who
say that what has just happened in Chile gives the lie to
the thesis of the people's war, to the validity of the armed
struggle, shall we say, elsewhere?

Allende: I said it just before our victory. The revolutionary struggle may be found in the guerrilla *foco* or in
urban insurrection; it may be the people's war and it may
be an insurgence through the polling booths; it depends
on the content it is given. In some countries, there is no
alternative to the armed struggle: where there are no
parties, no trade unions, where there is dictatorship, who
is going to believe in the possibility of an electoral victory?
There, elections offer no hope. And those people, these
revolutionaries, have to reach their objective.

Debray: Personally, I have seen and felt your victory
as an encouragement to continue the struggle, come what
may.

Allende: Of course, that's the right interpretation to
put on it.

Debray: With my very short political experience and
my slender knowledge of Latin America, I have noticed
that there are many Governments here which describe
themselves as revolutionary. But there are some that say

more than they do, and others, very few, that do more than they say. Here, one has the impression that one is dealing with one of the latter category.

Allende: We set a lot more store by actions than by words here.

Debray: Then, there probably remains little more for us to say. One last question, though: on the basis of experience in Chile, with the people's victory in Chile behind you, how do you see the future of Latin America?

Allende: Victory or no victory, I have always said the same thing. Latin America is an active volcano. The living death of the people cannot continue. As you well know, there are 120 million semi-illiterate and illiterate people on this Continent; as you know, there is a housing shortage in Latin America – 19 million dwellings; 70% of the people are ill-fed; as you know, our peoples are potentially very rich, and yet unemployment, hunger, ignorance, mental and physical misery are commonplace. The peoples of Latin America have no alternative but to struggle – each nation according to its circumstances – but struggle they must. For what? To win their economic independence and become nations that are completely free politically as well. Now, I believe that this is the great prospect that awaits us, and as President, I can say, to the young especially, that the great prospect and the great opportunity lies in this struggle, in rebellion, in dedication to solidarity with the workers. This Continent must achieve its political independence; we must prepare the way through economic independence. One day, Latin America will speak as a Continent with the voice of a united people, a voice which will be heard and respected, because it will be the voice of a people which is master of its own destiny. This is what I think, Régis, and I believe that you, comrade, can help our cause a great deal by telling people what you have seen and what we are striving for.

Debray: I shall try to do so. But now, I will not take up any more of your time, comrade. Thank you.

Notes

1

The Communist Party

Founded in January 1922 at a congress of the Socialist Workers' Party which changed its name and which had in turn been founded in 1912 by Luis Emilio Recabarren, pioneer of Chilean workers' struggles. The Communist Party was a member of the Third International. The Eighth Party Congress in January 1927 established its doctrinal basis, proclaiming: 'The party will strengthen the process of bolshevization. Communists do not enter Parliament in order to consecrate the capitalist regime, but to destroy it. The proletariat's emancipation will be achieved, not by democratic but by revolutionary methods. Its liberation lies not in Parliament but in the soviets.' This congress was almost the Party's last activity before Ibañez (*see note* 3) assumed power and its militants were heavily repressed and persecuted.

With the emergence of the Fourth International the party suffered a split. It joined the Popular Front which carried the Pedro Aguirre Cerda government (*see note* 6) into power, but later broke with it.

During Gonzales Videla's government – 1946–52 (*see note* 24) – the Communist Party entered the cabinet but was soon outlawed by a legal device – the Law in Defence of Democracy, the so-called 'Accursed Law'. Its leaders were deported, imprisoned and persecuted, but this did not prevent the party from continuing clandestine political activity, even mobilizing support for the first presidential candidacy of Salvador Allende in 1952. When the ban on the party was lifted in 1958 it returned to legality and the same year joined other left-wing forces in the Frente de Accion Popolar (Popular Action Front) which supported Allende's second presidential candidacy. The Communist Party has shown steady electoral growth ever since until in the last election it polled some 17 per cent of the vote.

Its presidential 'pre-candidate' at the Popular Unity Convention in 1969 was the poet, Pablo Neruda. The Communist Party has three ministers in Allende's cabinet, the Exchequer, Public Works and Labour; all of them are workers.

Socialist Party

Founded on 19 April 1933, though the antecedents of its foundation must be sought in a series of small socialist movements which had supported the *coup d'état* of Grove and Matte (*see note* 2) the year before. The declaration of principles at the party's foundation stated: 'The Party adheres to Marxism as the method for interpreting reality and recognizes the class struggle as the motive force of history.' The party's formation was the product of objective national conditions: the maturity of the working class, which already had a long tradition of struggle; the inability of the traditional parties to express the workers' interests; and also the crisis of leadership suffered by the proletariat, since, although the Communist Party had penetrated the Chilean working class, it was at that time split into two irreconcilable factions.

Moreover, the new party maintained certain differences with the Communist Party. A well-known Socialist Party theoretician summed these up as follows: 'Neither were the militants represented by the Communist Party whose too rigid ideological outlines, whose obedience to world strategy, and whose tactic of schematic slogans could not efficiently serve the spontaneous demands of the working class.'

The Party criticized the Second and Third Internationals, maintained its distance from them, and limited its international policies to a continental scale. Thus its declaration of principles proclaimed: 'The socialist doctrine is international in character and demands solidarity and coordinated action by workers throughout the world. In order to begin realizing these principles the Socialist Party will defend the economic and political unity of the people of the Continent to attain a Continental Federation of Socialist Republics and create an anti-imperialist economy.' On the question of state power, it adds: 'During the process of totally transforming the system, a dictatorship of organized workers is necessary.'

In the last parliamentary elections, the Socialist Party obtained nearly 15 per cent of the total vote.*

2

The Socialist Republic of Marmaduke Grove

The capitulation to imperialism and the political repression of the Ibañez dictatorship (1931) (*see note* 3) followed by the class rule of Montero (1932), had left behind a wave of social discontent expressed in strikes and other political actions by embryonic workers' organizations and left-wing political parties.

Tenacious political work by a number of socialist groups, combined with the discontent of the masses and the injustices committed by those in power, brought victory to a revolutionary movement led by Colonel Marmaduke Grove (military leader) and Eugenio Matte (civil leader). On 4 June 1932 President Montero was ousted and a socialist government was established.

With a 150 point programme and under the slogan 'Bread, a Roof and Shelter' the new government embarked on a series of concrete measures in favour of the dispossessed. Viewed today these measures appear extraordinarily ingenuous and naïve – suspension of evictions of tenants, the return of objects pledged to the Popular

---

* *Publisher's Note:* In the municipal elections of 5 April 1971 the Socialist Party received 22.38% of the votes. In the same elections the Christian Democrats received 25.62% and the Communists 16.97% of the votes. The Popular Unity together received 49.73% of the vote as against 48.05% for the divided opposition. In a senate by-election at the same time, the Socialist candidate Adonis Sepulveda, contesting the seat in Southern Chile which Salvador Allende had to vacate on assuming the presidency, received 52% of the votes.

Credit Bank, the granting of popular credits to small traders, etc. – but they undoubtedly provoked the immediate anger of the reactionary right. Moreover, the new government was clearly anti-imperialist: its economic programme stated that 'we have been deprived of the administration of credit, control of external and internal trade, control over wages and of the market. All heavy industry extracting primary products and a large part of the public services are in the hands of foreign enterprises. Our privileged classes have lived in the lap of luxury and comfort provided by foreign capitalism, in exchange for our natural wealth and the misery of the people. Thus the upstart bourgeoisie of Chile has shown less respect for all that is national than that in any other country which calls itself free'.

The programme of the revolutionaries did not attempt either the socialization of the means of production or the confiscation of great fortunes. Moreover, the government did not rely decisively on the masses to carry through its programme. It was therefore overthrown after twelve days by a *coup d'état* supported by the national bourgeoisie and imperialism. But there is no doubt that, despite its short duration, the Revolutionary Junta was an inspiration for the working class; and it united behind it five small socialist movements which fused the following year to found the Socialist Party (*see note* 1).

3

Carlos Ibañez del Campo

Ibañez was born in 1877, became an Army general, and was a personality in Chilean political life for thirty years. He first stood for the Presidency of the Republic in 1927, obtained 98 per cent of the votes and formed the government known as 'the Ibañez Dictatorship' (1927–1931).

In spite of the fact that he devoted his whole life to politics and was first and foremost a politician, Ibañez never worked in any political party but was constantly involved in the politics of personal conspiracy, participating in numerous 'palace coups'. It is said of him that between 1925 and 1940 'the only time one could be sure Ibañez was not conspiring was when he was President'.

Although his first government left unhappy memories of authoritarianism and political persecution, Ibañez was put forward as a presidential candidate in 1951 by a conglomeration of independent forces – a party specially created for the occasion (the Agrarian Labour Party) and one wing of the Socialist Party (the Popular Socialist Party).

His platform had a populist-demagogic character and was based on the need for moral rectitude and for cleaning up the management of 'public life'.

In an election in which there were three other candidates (including Salvador Allende who was standing for the first time, backed by the Communists and one wing of the Socialists) Ibañez obtained an overwhelming majority of the votes, nearly 50 per cent.

His thoroughly reactionary economic policy included the bringing to Chile of a North American mission (the Klein-Sacks mission) which gave total control over his economic policies to the International Monetary Fund. This brought about the departure from the government of the Popular Socialist Party. Far from being able to halt inflation, Ibañez accelerated it and his policy of 'moral reform' was not put into practice by the government, in which all kinds of irregularities occurred.

The Ibañez government established links with Perón's populist regime in Argentina. A series of mutual friendship and good-will communiqués culminated in a notorious visit to Chile by Perón in 1953. The political purposes of this alliance are not clear, but there began to be talk of a military-populist axis between Chile and Argentina with the intention of establishing leadership of and hegemony over the continent.

At the end of his term of office Ibañez repealed the Defence of Democracy Law which had outlawed the Communist Party for ten years. This enabled the party to mobilize support for Allende in his second presidential candidacy in 1958. Carlos Ibañez died in 1960.

4

Lautarian and Masonic Lodges

The Lautarian Lodges (or Lautaro's Lodges), named after the Araucanian *cacique* Lautaro – leader of the struggle against the Spanish Conquest in sixteenth-century Chile – were created in Buenos Aires in 1812 by members of the Freemasonry. Prominent among them were General José San Martín and Bernardo O'Higgins in Chile, both leaders of the struggle against Spanish colonialism. It is said that while the Army formed the military wing of the liberation movement, Lautaro's Lodges constituted its political wing. This is corroborated by the fact that San Martín and O'Higgins took pains to create Lodges in the territories newly entered by the Andes Liberation Army. The fundamental aims of the Lodges have been defined as civic indoctrination and the study of the political and social potentialities of the embryonic nation. The relationship between the Lautarian and the Masonic Lodges has been described by an historian as follows: 'Since initiation in the mysteries of freemasonry was obligatory for all affiliates of Lautaro's Lodges, we can affirm that if the objectives of the Lodge were clearly political, their members were equally clearly masonic.' Thus the first masonic lodge in Chile, created on 15 March 1827, had its roots in Lautaro's Lodges, and its first Grand Master was Manuel Blanco Encalada who had also been a member of a Lautarian Lodge. The connections between both Lodges are evident in their use of common symbols and rituals and also in the similarity of their functions and activities. The following paragraph from the statutes of Lautaro's Lodge of Chile, written by Bernardo O'Higgins himself, corroborates the above: 'Whenever any of the brothers is elected to the Supreme Government he must not decide anything of great importance without consulting the lodge . . .', and, he added, '. . . by virtue of the objectives of the institution, one of the primary obligations of the brothers will be to assist and protect each other in any civil conflict and support each others' opinion'. Moreover, '. . . any brother who breaks the secrecy of the lodge's existence, even with a word or sign, will be punishable by death, by the means thought most convenient . . .'.

5

The Radical Party

The Radical Party was formed by a group of members of the Liberal Party who broke away under the leadership of Pedro Leon Gallo in 1858. The party's basic principles, formulated at the 1888 Congress were: the separation of the state from the church; the establishment of obligatory, free, lay primary education; improvement in the legal status of women. These were very advanced reforms for the ruling oligarchy and ascendant bourgeoisie of that epoch. The Radical Party's reformist attitude towards the masses can be summed up in the phrase of one of its most brilliant members of that time, Enrique MacIver, for whom 'the workers lack the necessary culture and preparation for understanding the problems of government, let alone constituting part of it'.

As a political entity, the Radical Party expressed the hopes of a growing 'middle class' whose interests it represented. Its most serious differences with the oligarchy stemmed from religious and educational questions, on which the Radical Party's attitude was more advanced.

In the twentieth century the party has reached the Government through various political coalitions and the presidency of the country between 1938 and 1952 was successively held by three of its members. In 1969, supported by the rank and file, the party's most progressive wing won control, and threw out the most reactionary faction which had held the leadership during the period of its coalition with the right wing. Implementing the resolutions of the congress of that year, the party encouraged the formation of 'Popular Unity' and became part of the popular government with three ministers.

6

Pedro Aguirre Cerda and the Popular Front

After the Seventh Congress of the Comintern in 1935, the Chilean Communist Party devoted itself entirely to agitating for the formation of a Popular Front, an idea that found an echo in a large sector of the Radical Party. This line was based on the struggle against fascism and in defence of democracy. In the words of an historian of Chilean socialism, Julio César Jobet: 'The Popular Front came into being as an alliance of worker and bourgeois-democratic forces with a programme which tended to eliminate the extreme antagonisms between the classes. Its main points were the defence of democratic liberties as well as some economic and social reforms in view of the poverty-stricken conditions of the working masses.' The Popular Front was formed in 1936 and it immediately clashed with the nationalist right wing strongly unified around one of its characteristic figures, Gustavo Ross Santa María.

In 1938 the Convention of the Left chose the radical teacher, Pedro Aguirre Cerda as the candidate representing the Popular Front in the Presidential election of that year.

The election campaign, which ended in a 4,000 vote victory for Aguirre Cerda, involved an extremely sharp struggle against resistance from the Right. In addition to the Radical Party, which was the principal force in the coalition, the Communist Party, the Socialist Party, the Democratic Party and some Ibañist groups supported Aguirre Cerda. The government's programme was basically reformist, promulgating a series of measures designed to develop and make more flexible a national economy seriously compromised by foreign interests. The most important reform was undoubtedly the creation of the Corporation for the Development of Production, whose basic mission was rapid industrialization of the country through economic planning and the control of industrial credit.

Just when the idea of the Popular Front had lost its world-wide significance, Aguirre Cerda died, on 23 November 1941.

7

Victor Raul Haya de la Torre and the APRA

Haya de la Torre emerged as a student leader in Peru in 1918 participating in the one-day demonstration in support of an eight-hour day. In 1923 he was deported to Mexico, where he founded the Alianza Popular Revolucionaria Americana (APRA). The central concern of the party at its birth was a thorough agrarian reform and the destruction of the big estates and the oligarchy. It planned the creation of a state with a strong nationalist image. For that epoch, APRA constituted the most advanced expression of thought in Peru. Nevertheless, by defending an alliance of classes in the anti-imperialist struggle, Haya de la Torre represented the purest form of bourgeois social reformism.

By winning support among the masses he was able to dominate parliament and make Bustamente President in 1945. In 1948, APRA rebelled against Bustamente in an effort to take full power but, after violent struggles, the military led by Odría seized power, initiating a dictatorship which brought eight years of harsh repression against APRA. Haya de la Torre took refuge in the Colombian embassy where he remained for most of the Odría dictatorship. From this time APRA began to decline, initiating a series of alliances with the bourgeoisie including its old enemies the military.

Juan José Arevalo

Arevalo was a Guatemalan politician exiled to Argentina by Ubico's dictatorship (1931–45). With Ubico's downfall, he was called to lead a broad reformist movement.

After winning power he drew up the Political Constitution of 1946, the first after two long periods of dictatorship. He wrote a famous anti-imperialist book, *The Fable of the Shark and the Sardines*, and helped raise the anti-imperialist consciousness of his people. He encouraged the formation of trade unions, and under his government for the first time in Guatemalan history a series of political parties were organized – among them the Guatemalan Workers' Party, in 1947.

Arevalo was the first elected president to complete his term of office (from 1946 to 1952), and he was followed by Jacobo Arbenz, also elected by popular ballot. Arbenz radicalized the social reform movement before being deposed by a military coup and invasion supported and financed by the CIA in June 1954.

Romulo Betancourt and Democratic Action

A Venezuelan politician, Betancourt began as a student leader in 1926. Two years later, exiled to Costa Rica, he joined a Marxist-Leninist group and was expelled from the country as a 'communist'. His first analysis of Venezuela pointed out that the 'imperialist international' needed to maintain repressive governments in his country 'in order to place its means of production in the service of foreign exploitation'. On his return to Venezuela in 1936, Betancourt organized the National Democratic Party. Its legalization was blocked by López Contrera's government, which accused it of being 'communist'. In 1937 Betancourt was again deported. He made good use of his time by organizing an international campaign for the democratization of Venezuela, for the independence of Puerto Rico, and against militarism and imperialism. In this period he visited Chile for the first time and made contact with socialist forces participating in the Popular Front. On 13 September 1941 Democratic Action, an anti-imperialist, agrarian party, was born with Betancourt as its leader. It profited from the new conditions created in Venezuela by the government of Isaías Medina Angarita which, in 1943, enforced a new petroleum law and later a conservative programme of agrarian reform. Democratic Action was in opposition from 1944 and on 18 October 1945 participated in the *coup d'état* which overthrew Medina. The movement was led by young officers – among them Carlos Delgado Chalbaud and Marcos Pérez Jimenez. A junta was formed in which Betancourt participated as President. In December 1947 elections were held, bringing victory to the writer Rómulo Gallegos, candidate of Democratic Action. He was overthrown by a *coup d'état* ten months after assuming power. Colonel Adams of the North American Mission actively participated in the *coup* which gave power to Pérez Jimenez, Delgado Chalbaud (subsequently assassinated) and Llovera Páez. Betancourt returned to exile. After seizing power with North American support, Pérez Jimenez was decorated by Eisenhower in 1954 and maintained his position until he was toppled by a mass movement in January 1958. Elections were held that year and Betancourt and his party won them. Only the Communist Party remained in opposition, repudiated by Betancourt himself in exchange for the support of the bourgeoisie and imperialism. In August 1959 police gun-fire dispersed a demonstration of the unemployed in Caracas. This started a wave of repression against independent trade unions and the Communist Party, taking a toll of more than fifty victims by 1962 when the Armed Forces of National Liberation (FALN) was born, initiating the armed struggle in Venezuela. The FALN and its political organization, the National Liberation Front, was in large measure a result of the efforts of the Communist Party which had decided to take up arms against the repressive, pro-imperialist government of Betancourt. This government, praised by Kennedy, is remembered as one of the most sinister in

Venezuela's history. Nevertheless, Betancourt was able to last out his period of presidential office and transfer power to his successor, Raúl Leoni, also a member of Democratic Action. At present he is again preparing to offer himself as a candidate, hoping to replace the Christian Socialist, Rafael Caldera.

8
Augusto César Sandino

In 1925 Sandino organized armed struggle against the North American occupation of his country, Nicaragua. With a guerrilla detachment, he established a strong position in Las Segovias, a forest zone of the country. The struggle of Sandino and his men against a vastly superior enemy became a legend throughout Latin America. In 1927 the United States sent a landing force to Nicaragua in sixteen warships. The force was commanded by Brigadier General Logan Feland, who was decorated by President Coolidge after the aerial bombardment of El Ocotal – where Sandino was supposed to be hiding – in which three hundred Nicaraguans and one North American lost their lives. The struggle dragged on until 1933 when the United States withdrew its forces. Sandino made peace with the new government. However, as he was leaving the Presidential Palace, he was trapped in an ambush and assassinated by the Chief of the National Guard, Anastasio Somoza, who subsequently revealed that the order was given by the American Ambassador himself, Arthur Bliss Lane. The name of Augusto César Sandino is frequently invoked in Latin America as the first anti-imperialist fighter to take up the armed struggle.

9
Carlos Rafael Rodriguez

Member of the Secretariat of the Cuban Communist Party, Minister in the Revolutionary Government. In

November 1970 Rodriguez led the Cuban delegation to Chile on the occasion of the transfer of Presidential power. In December 1970 Cuba and Chile renewed diplomatic relations, broken since 1964 when Jorge Alessandri obeyed the order of the OAS at Punta del Este, designed to isolate Cuba from its brother countries of Latin America.

10

Salvador Allende and the Guerrilla Fighters
(Easter Island, Tahiti)

On 17 February 1968, a cable from La Paz indicated that a group of five guerrilla fighters (three Cubans and two Bolivians), the last survivors from the Bolivian guerrilla led by Ernesto Che Guevara, had crossed the Bolivian-Chilean frontier. The revolutionaries had travelled more than 1,400 kilometres to reach Chile from Oruro, without food, poorly equipped, and implacably persecuted by the army and the Bolivian Rangers with whom they had fought on two occasions before reaching freedom. When the news arrived in Santiago, the press, the Parliamentary Left and the government immediately made preparations. A series of spontaneous demonstrations and gatherings of support took place in different parts of the country. Three thousand people demonstrated in Iquique where the guerrilla fighters had given themselves up to the authorities. Allende, at that time President of the Senate, was one of the first to move to the northern zone in order to ensure that proper protection was granted to the victims of political persecution, and that they received the maximum of medical and other facilities. While the revolutionaries were submitted to medical checks and police interrogation, left wing members of parliament held discussions with the government to have them brought quickly to Santiago. Once this was done, the government issued a decree expelling the revolutionaries from Chilean territory, and sent them at once to Easter Island on a special National

Airline flight. The revolutionaries left Santiago very early in the morning, guarded by intelligence agents, without the representatives of the Chilean Left being informed of the time of their departure or their destination. In this situation Allende spoke personally to the Minister of the Interior, and in his capacity as President of the Senate insisted on taking the plane for Easter Island, determined to witness and guarantee the undisturbed journey of the revolutionaries to Tahiti and then to Havana, via Europe. Allende also saw his journey as an act of ideological and human solidarity by a representative of the Chilean Left towards a group of combatants who had fought beside Commandante Guevara in his last moments as the leader of the guerrilla in Bolivia's liberation movement. Allende stayed with the guerrilla fighters on Easter Island and travelled with them to Tahiti until they left for Europe.

On his return to Santiago, Allende faced the most inflammatory campaign in the reactionary press which thought it could use his journey of solidarity to eliminate him from political life. But Allende was able to counterattack when he was invited to participate in a television forum with the editors of the papers that had led the defamatory campaign. There Allende changed from accused into accuser, explaining his actions as the political consequences of his whole life. For a 'militant of the Latin American revolution,' he said, 'to extend his human and ideological solidarity to comrades fighting in the same revolution is a legitimate and honourable duty', 'something that all revolutionaries accept, but that lackeys and mercenaries will never understand.' His whole intervention was a sharp criticism of the mass media, an attack against mercenary journalism and against the system and the political groups which maintain and direct it. At the same time, it constituted a clear summary of the political situation and of the revolutionary possibilities, as well as of his own position in Chilean politics. The following paragraph, replying to the director of the conservative Chilean paper *El Mercurio*, is a good example of Allende's inter-

vention: 'Up till now Chile has been a bourgeois democratic country; despite all faults, it is indisputably one of
the countries of Latin America in which non-military
struggles still have a real meaning. But the possibility of
the popular movement in Chile winning a victory through
the ballot box is being increasingly reduced, and one of
the chief culprits is *El Mercurio* with its shameful, im-
placable and never-ending distortions of the truth and of
the facts, its relentless defence of its own interests, its
refusal to allow the immense majority of Chileans a different life. As for us, no one is going to dictate our path,
just as no one – no socialist party, no socialist country –
has dictated the path of the Chilean popular movement.
We regret that violence is being increasingly unleashed
on the world, but it is a fact of imperialism. You cannot
get away from the fact of Vietnam, Vietnam which does
not exist for *El Mercurio* although it even exists for the
Pope in his capacity as a human being. Struggles are
going to develop and on a global and continental
scale; as a Chilean, I earnestly hope that we escape
violence; nevertheless, when one sees the plans for creating an inter-American peace force, when one knows the
ideological frontiers, when one considers how the Americans invaded Santo Domingo, what the Americans have
done in Brazil, what they are doing in their own country,
then one must seriously doubt that they will respect the
will of the people. For that reason I remain in the popular
struggle and I repeat to you that we will not initiate
violence, but that revolutionary violence is sometimes the
only answer to your violence, the violence of the reactionaries.'

11

MAPU *(Movement of United Popular Action)*

MAPU was formed when the most progressive section of
the Christian Democratic Party, mainly the youth, broke
away following an agitated party Congress in 1968. One

of the non-Marxist movements of Popular Unity, it has directed its efforts and its most experienced cadres towards political action in the countryside.

As Christians committed to the revolutionary process, MAPU proposed Jacques Chonchol, now Minister of Agriculture, as their pre-candidate at the Popular Unity round-table discussions which chose Salvador Allende as the standard bearer of the united left.

Besides the Agriculture Minister, a woman militant of the Movement has been appointed Minister of Family Welfare, a ministry which is being formed at present.

Social Democratic Party

The Social Democratic Party was founded in July 1966 by a deputy called Patricio Hurtado who broke from the Christian Democrats and Frei's government. He united the Movement of National Rebellion (MORENA) with the group called the National Democratic Party, whose leader is Senator Luis Fernando Luengo.

The Social Democratic Party defines itself as a national movement committed to the process of Latin American liberation and to solidarity with the Cuban Revolution. According to its leader, Patricio Hurtado, it bears no relation to international Social Democracy nor to traditional social democratic concepts.

API (*Independent Popular Action*)

API is the smallest of the political forces within the Popular Unity and has the shortest history. Its leader, Rafael Tarud, is a Senator and current president of the National Command of the Popular Unity. The present Minister of Justice is an active member of this movement.

12

The CUT *(The Single Workers' Union)*

The CUT groups together the confederations, federations, groups and guild centres which voluntarily accept its principles and statutes. It was created on 12 February 1953 after a long period of divisions which had developed in the Chilean workers' movement following the break-up of the Chilean Workers' Federation in 1946. Thus, from its inception the CUT reincarnated the best revolutionary traditions of the old Chilean Workers' Federation (FOCR) founded by Luis Emilio Recabarren, the pioneer of workers' struggles in the country (*see note* 1). Its first declaration of principles set out the aim of replacing the oppressor state with socialism through the militant struggles of the Chilean workers. Because of its militancy, its leaders were severely repressed for a long time (1953–1961), particularly its President, Clotario Blest, who was persecuted, imprisoned and exiled on many occasions. But, at its first Congress in 1957, the CUT started to question its first declaration of principles, which was finally altered in December 1959 in favour of something more tepid, which concentrated on economic and social demands without questioning the political foundations of the system.

The change was basically due to pressures in this period from centrist sectors allied to the Christian Democratic and Radical Parties. From that time onwards successive national congresses – 1962, 1965, 1968 – changed its political line and it is now one of the organizations which firmly supports the popular government.

The organizational structure of the CUT is as follows: it is governed by a National Executive Council composed of thirty-five members elected by universal, secret ballot. This Council sits for three-year periods, being re-elected at each Congress, and it includes the President, two Vice-Presidents, the General Secretary, the Treasurer, etc. Under the National Executive Council are Regional, Departmental, District and local councils and the trade unions, the latter forming the base of the organization.

Parallel to this structure is the National Executive Council of Federations, which consists of the National Executive Council plus delegates from the Federations, which number about forty. It has been the popular parties which have maintained leadership within the organization since its foundation. Thus, its current President is Luis Figueroa, a Communist Deputy, and its General Secretary is Hernàn del Canto, a member of the Central Committee of the Socialist Party. Although the CUT is the most representative organ of the Chilean working class, the constitution does not give it legal recognition, and it is therefore only a *de facto* organization. This prevents it carrying out collective contracts, buying or selling goods, or carrying out any other act with a legal status. This situation has lingered on since the promulgation of the Labour Code of 1925, which explicitly forbids the formation of Trade Union Confederations and recognizes the existence only of individual trade unions at the factory or company level. But the CUT's *de facto* existence and influence over the working class led to its being mentioned in many subsequent Labour laws. When the popular government assumed power, it sent a bill to Congress establishing the CUT's juridical status for the first time in its history. The right wing, in alliance with the Christian Democrats, made use of a chance parliamentary majority to reject the bill.

This rejection is clearly not based on solid legal grounds and the official explanation given is that the CUT, which embraces only about twenty per cent of all Chilean workers, should not be allowed to collect dues from all the workers in the country. In fact the reason is political: legal recognition plus the consequent financial autonomy would enable the CUT to become one of the most powerful organizations in the country; this the right wing obviously cannot stomach.

13

The Bicameral Congress

The Chilean Bicameral Congress was created by the Constitution of 1822 and consolidated by that of 1833. Modelled on the Roman System, it was originally composed of a Senate with a moderating and elder-statesman-like character, and a Chamber with fiscal control over the actions of the Executive. The present constitution of 1925 stripped the Senate of the political role it had hitherto possessed and transformed it into a High Court and a consultative body. The Senate has no fiscal powers; it is only a second wing of the legislature with the functions of a court in specified cases.

Both Senators and Deputies are directly elected. The only difference in the qualifications required to be able to stand for these two chambers is that of age: a deputy must be over twenty-one years old; a Senator must be over thirty-five. The Chamber of Deputies consists of one hundred and fifty members elected every four years; the Senate consists of fifty members who sit for eight years, being partially renewed every four years.

14

Assassination of René Schneider

At 8.15 a.m. on 22 October 1970, as the Commander-in-Chief of the Army, René Schneider was travelling to his office at the Ministry of Defence, his car was intercepted by eight vehicles from which several armed men emerged. They proceeded to break the windows of the general's car and, when he resisted, they fired three shots, hitting him in the throat, the thorax, and the right shoulder. The assassins fled while the general was driven by his chauffeur to the Military Hospital where, after three days in acute pain, he died on the morning of 25 October.

Subsequent investigations of the event brought to light far-reaching seditious plans, of which the foiled kidnapping of the general was only an initial step, designed to block the ratification of Allende's electoral triumph by the Congress two days later. The first to be arrested were young people from wealthy families who had political connections with right-wing parties. At the same time, a number of ultra right-wing organizations (The Alessandri Legion, 'Don't Surrender Chile', 'The Nationalist Offensive', and the 'Independent Republican Front') were to further the plot by carrying out terrorist actions in different parts of Santiago.

General Schneider's death created an uproar in the country, for a political assassination had not occurred since the last century (Diego Portales's assassination in 1837). According to Allende, if the original plan to kidnap the general had succeeded, the country could have been driven towards civil war. At the present moment, the number of people arrested or declared guilty in connection with this case has risen to thirty-two, including generals, one admiral, big estate owners and political personalities.

15

Jorge Alessandri Rodriguez

Civil engineer, ex-deputy, ex-Senator, and ex-Chancellor of the Exchequer, Alessandri was President of the Republic between 1958 and 1964. His father was twice President of the Republic. Alessandri has also been President of the Confederation of Commerce and Production, the leading organization of the industrial and commercial bourgeoisie. A prominent businessman – member and chairman of many limited companies – he is the most typical representative of the Chilean economic and political right wing, although he has never been active in any political party.

His government, which lasted six years, is remembered as one of the most reactionary in the last three decades. Nevertheless, at the age of seventy-four he was put forward by the right-wing in the last presidential elections as the symbol of independent, national regeneration.

16

MIR – CP (*The Incident at Concepción*)

This was an incident in which Oscar Arnoldo Ríos, a twenty-three-year-old student at Concepción University and a militant in the Movement of the Revolutionary Left (MIR), was shot during a clash with members of the Communist Youth, on 2 December 1970. The clash coincided with negotiations to draw up a single left-wing list for the presidential and executive elections of the student federation at Concepción University.

Ríos's death marked the culmination of a long period of ideological disputes which had driven those involved into sectarian positions. It was also the main factor in stimulating the revision and self-criticism of these positions and in showing the need for an open dialogue as the only method of agreement in the struggle against the main enemy: the national bourgeoisie and imperialism. The first consequence of this approach was the creation of a single left-wing list, headed by a MIR militant whom the Communists supported. At the time of the incident, President Allende was on board a ship of the Chilean Navy, travelling to Valparaiso. He played a decisive role in promoting, stimulating and speeding up this dialogue, thus preventing political gains being made by the right and by Christian Democracy and avoiding a fratricidal fight among the Chilean popular and revolutionary forces. The MIR – CP dialogue is continuing at top level and is considered by Chilean observers to be the main political factor in the union of the forces of the left.

17

The CUP (*Committees of Popular Unity*)

These were mass organizations created by the Popular Unity in order to channel and advance mass participation in the election campaign.

Of various sizes, the Committees were created 'in factories, shanty towns, offices, schools, etc.'. According to the Popular Unity Programme, their function is 'to prepare for the exercise of political power'. At the same time, they constitute '. . . a permanent and dynamic force for carrying out its programme, an active school for the masses and a concrete organization through which the political content of Popular Unity can be deepened at all levels.'

The work of the CUPs reached its culminating point immediately before and after the election. Recently, the Popular Government made a call to all these committees to maintain themselves in readiness to confront any seditious provocations from the reactionaries.

18

Cautín

An agrarian province in South Chile with the only important concentration of Indians in the country: it has 190,000 Mapuches representing 75% of its total population. But they own only 25% of the cultivable land: this means one and a half hectares for each Indian, of which only 60% is cultivable. Although the province provides 24% of national milk production, 18% of meat production and 25% of wheat, it is one of the most underdeveloped regions in the country: 37% of the Mapuches are illiterate; 20,000 are unemployed; they have the highest infant mortality rate, and they are notably deficient in medical services.

It is in this region that fifty-six seizures of rural property have been carried out by the Indian peasants over the last six months, using the method of 'fence enclosure'. There were even armed clashes with the latifundists who, after Salvador Allende's victory, organized themselves into strongly armed 'white guards'. On their side the Indians have also achieved a high degree of political organization under the leadership of the Revolutionary Peasant Movement. Thus, in the Lautaro Commune, the collectives are trying to convert their zone into a single wheat producing commune organized on a socialist basis. In fact, in three collectives socialist forms of life and work are being put in practice, entailing a great ideological change for the mapuche. The reactionary right has carried out armed attacks against the Indians who have tried to recover the lands usurped from them. The peasants have shown organization and determination in the face of these provocations, and the class struggle is therefore more visible and violent in Cautín than in any other part of present-day Chile. Against this background the government has intervened, sending the Minister of Agriculture to the area to speed up programmes of agrarian reform and social development.

19

Raúl Morales' Parliamentary Immunity

On 21 November 1970, the Military Prosecutor, Fernando Lyon, demanded the lifting of Senator Raúl Morales Adriasola's parliamentary immunity – Morales is a member of the right-wing Radical Democratic Party – in order that he could be interrogated. Those convicted of breaking the internal security of the state and of assassinating the Commander-in-Chief of the Army, General René Schneider (*see note* 14), had made statements implicating him in the affair. The gist of these statements was that the right-wing Senator appeared to be the co-ordinator of an ambitious plan of sedition which included bringing five hundred machine-guns from Argentina in order to create chaos and eventually overthrow the Popular Government.

The demand for the lifting of immunity was approved in the first instance by the Court of Appeal. But the Supreme Court over-ruled the Appeal Court's decision – a ruling which caused national consternation. The affair both confirmed the political nature of the Supreme Court's decisions and obstructed the normal course of investigation, for the Military Prosecutor remained unable to call on the Senator to make a statement.

20

The Carabineros

A uniformed, militarized police force, under the Ministry of the Interior's control, whose basic function is the maintenance of internal security and law and order.

The Carabineros were formed through the unification and centralization of the different local and provincial police forces and militias, under General Ibañez's first government in 1927 (see note 3). It now constitutes a professional corps, equipped with modern, heavy armaments, communication, transport and an efficient bureaucratic organization. It comprises 30,000 men, distributed all over the country and organized in specialized units. The General Director of the Carabineros is answerable only to the President of the Republic.

Mobile Carabinier Group

This unit was created in 1960 and specialized in the repression of worker, student and peasant movements. It had modern equipment and its members received special training. It became nearly 2,000 strong and was the most efficient repressive instrument at the disposal of the Alessandri and Frei governments. One of President Allende's Popular Government's first measures was the abolition of this repressive body in November 1970.

21

The Defence Counsel of the State

This is the public body responsible for giving legal counsel to the Executive and for legal defence of the state's fiscal interests in all matters dealt with in the courts in which the State or the State Treasury are involved. It is composed of twelve eminent professional lawyers, and its views on any juridical problem constitute the last word. At present its head is Eduardo Novoa, a respected lawyer of the independent left, who has belonged to the Council for about thirty years.

22

San Miguel and Puerto Montt

San Miguel: In 1968 a group of peasants struck for a series of demands that were ignored by the bosses. After thirty-nine days of legal strike and after all legal means of negotiation had been exhausted, they seized and held the 'San Miguel' estate. The Frei government's Ministry of the Interior dispatched 600 men and six armoured-cars of the Mobile Group (*see note* 20) to evict them. The entire group of peasants was imprisoned and tried for subversion. *Puerto Montt:* One hundred families of unemployed seized some private, unenclosed and unused land situated two kilometres from Puerto Montt with the intention of obtaining some land to live on. After a week of peaceful occupation, at 5 a.m. on Sunday, 9 March 1969, the Ministry of the Interior sent 200 troops of the Mobile Group, strongly armed with tear-gas, rifles, machine-guns and petrol, to dislodge the settlers and set fire to their huts. When the settlers tried to resist, the Mobile Group advanced firing its automatic weapons. The official toll in this massacre was eight people dead and twenty-seven wounded.

23

Chuquicamata

The biggest open-face copper mine in the world which, until 1969, was totally owned by the North American Anaconda Copper Company through its Chilean branch, the Chile Exploration Company. That year the company reached an agreement with Frei's government, by which the Chilean State bought 51 per cent of the shares, forming a mixed society with the North American company. This agreement – which the Chilean left opposed – contained a so-called 'Law Contract' by which its annulment required the acceptance of both parties. This law is the juridical reason for the Popular Unity's plan, on assuming power, to implement constitutional reform in order to nationalize the copper industry; for this is the only juridical mechanism which would permit nationalization without entering into commercial agreements with North American companies. But there is a political as well as a juridical basis for making the reform bill a constitutional reform rather than a simple law: namely, just as a Constitution was drawn up to declare the country's political independence from Spanish colonialism, so a Constitutional reform will mark the economic independence of the country from foreign capital.

Chuquicamata's total production in 1970 was 262,998 metric tons of fine copper, which represents nearly half Chile's total output of fine copper.

24

Gabriel Gonzales Videla

A Radical politician who was President of the Republic from 1946 to 1952. As well as his own Radical Party, the Communist Party supported his election and entered his government for a year. However, under pressure from imperialism and the national bourgeoisie, he broke with the Communist Party on the grounds of supposed international conspiracy and promulgated a 'Law in Defence of Democracy', starting the bloody persecution of Communist militants (*see note* 1). The Law in Defence of Democracy was conceived as a means of suppressing and outlawing the Communist Party and is known by the Chilean working class as the 'Accursed Law'. It is perhaps the only act for which the frivolous and commonplace Gonzales Videla will be remembered. He put the country in debt and handed it over to foreign interests, betrayed the party which had carried him to power, and devoted himself to facile flattery of the bourgeoisie. On retirement from active politics he used these relationships to enter the banking business.

25

The Statue of Constitutional Guarantees

Although Salvador Allende, the Popular candidate, won the elections on 4 September 1970, he did not obtain an absolute majority. Thus, in accordance with the State Constitution, the Plenum of the Congress fifty days later had to choose between him and the right-wing runner-up, Jorge Alessandri. The votes of the Christian Democrats, whose candidate had only come third, would thus decide the outcome of the election fifty days later. From the start, the Christian Democratic Party's rank and file, especially the youth, had rejected the possibility of supporting the candidate of the right. But the party leadership supported the Popular Unity only on condition that it would approve a Statute of Constitutional Guarantees before the Plenary Congress took place; for, while the Christian Democracy did not distrust 'the democratic intentions of Salvador Allende, not everybody who supported him deserved the same trust'. The Statute of Guarantees is an assortment of legal points amending the political constitution of the State. Salvador Allende and the Popular Unity accepted the procedure and a joint commission – Christian Democracy and Popular Unity – was formed to draw up the constitutional amendments which comprise the Statute of Guarantees. According to the Christian Democrats, these amendments will secure the permanence of a democratic regime in Chile. Briefly, they consist of the following: guarantee of the freedom of political parties; protection of the freedom of the press, of the right of assembly, freedom of education; inviolability of correspondence; freedom of work; freedom of movement; assured social participation of groups in the community; professionalization of the Armed Forces and the Carabineros.

Only one of the points in the Statute was rejected outright by Allende and the Popular Unity. This was the one by which the Chilean Armed Forces were made the arbiter ensuring the fulfilment of the Statute. The Christian Democrats accepted this objection and the Statute was sent as a bill to the Congress which approved it in the first constitutional proceedings before the full Congress, which proclaimed Salvador Allende President of the Republic by 153 votes to 36.

26

Radomiro Tomic

Born in 1914, Tomic became a lawyer and university lecturer. With Frei and others, he founded the National Falange when a group of students split from the Conservative Party in 1933. After a Congress in 1956, the Falange became the present Christian Democratic Party. He started his public career as a journalist in Norte Grande. Later he became the Falange's first deputy in 1941 and was re-elected in 1945; he was twice a Senator, from 1950 to 1958 and from 1961 to 1 January 1965 when he left the Senate during Frei's government to assume the post of Ambassador to the USA. He returned from there in 1968 and in August 1969 was proclaimed his party's candidate for the Presidency of the Republic.

Although he had declared that without the support of the Popular Unity he would not remain a candidate, he finally revoked this original position, standing as the candidate only of the Christian Democratic Party.

Because his programme of social reforms was more bold and advanced than the one which had carried Frei into the Presidency in 1964, and because of a vigorous election campaign, he polled 800,000 votes and won third place. At present he leads the Christian left, the most progressive current within his party. Some of this sector's basic principles coincide with the government of Popular Unity's programme, and it is precisely these which separate it from the party's right wing led by Frei.

27

Organization of Latin American Solidarity (OLAS)

Conceived at the Tricontinental in Havana in January 1966, its first conference was held at the end of July 1967, and was attended by representatives from twenty-seven countries. Its political creed is based on the conception of continental armed struggle against North American imperialism. Its basic functions are solidarity with, co-ordination of, and support for national liberation struggles throughout the continent. The declaration of the closing session of the conference made a frontal attack on the reformist positions of some of the left-wing parties in Latin America, pointing out that 'the revolutionary armed struggle constitutes the fundamental line for the Latin American revolution'. Both the Communist and Socialist Parties of Chile were represented at the OLAS Conference, the former by Senators Volodia Teitelboim and Jorge Montes and the latter by Senator Carlos Altamirano and its leader Clodomiro Almeyda, present Minister of Foreign Affairs. Returning to Chile, where they faced a strong press campaign from the right and the Christian Democratic Party, they formed the Chilean branch of OLAS, headed by Senator Aniceto Rodriguez, then General Secretary of the Socialist Party. As in other countries, the OLAS Committee in Chile did not carry out any further activity.

APPENDIX

THE IMPLICATIONS OF THE ELECTORAL
RESULT FOR THE REVOLUTIONARY LEFT

Publisher's Note: This text is a shortened version of a policy statement, issued by the National Secretariat of the Movimiento di Izquierda Revolucionaria (MIR – *see note 16*) immediately following the electoral victory of 4 September 1970.

I INTRODUCTION

1. The electoral majority obtained by the Left has brought some confusion into the ranks of the Revolutionary Left, especially among its youngest militants and in its periphery.

At first sight the election triumph appears to be evidence of the failure of the strategy of armed struggle for seizing power in Chile; superficially, it also indicates that our non-participation in electoral activity was a political error and, subjectively, a triumph for the Reformist Left.

From this point of view our strategy (armed struggle, prolonged guerrilla warfare) our tactics (direct action, mass mobilization) and even our organizational policy, seem to be called in question.

2. Against this background, our militants are confronted by many concrete questions which require a speedy and clear answer. For example: what is the meaning of the Popular Unity's election victory? Has the strategy of armed struggle failed in Chile? Must revolutionaries unite with the Popular Unity government and unconditionally support it? Must we abandon our political-military form of organization? Must our forms of political action be abandoned? If an amnesty is granted, should the militants, at present working in illegality, return to legality? What political alliances should we make in this

period? How will we finance our organization? How far should we push mobilization to polarize the situation at the mass fronts?

II GENERAL OUTLINE

North American Imperialism and
the Latin American Bourgeoisie

Without going deeply into this problem, we must answer here one fundamental question posed for the Left after the election victory: can an alliance possibly be formed, at this time and in Chile, between important sectors of the national bourgeoisie and the traditional Left to develop an effective, anti-imperialist government policy?

1. The Latin American bourgeoisie, unlike those of Europe and North America, did not develop through its own efforts, but basically as the illegitimate daughter of foreign capital.

This relationship of dependence has not only been maintained but strengthened in the last decades. The Latin American ruling class is constituted by a social and political complex which embraces the North American ruling classes and our native bourgeoisie, whose economic, military and political interests are closely linked.

2. Secondary contradictions exist between imperialism and the national bourgeoisie, based on the struggle between them for the greatest share of what has been produced through the exploitation of Latin America. But their common interest in maintaining the system of exploitation and domination on which they base their power and wealth always prevails over these contradictions. They will thus always tighten their alliance and present a common front before the workers of every country.

3. The contradictions between the native bourgeoisie and imperialism will always grow sharper whenever the proportion of the spoils either of them acquires from exploitation declines significantly, and when the masses retreat or stand still, that is to say, do not threaten the system's survival.

For many years, development in Latin America, basically sustained through import substitution in the industrial sector, has stagnated, and the alternative of a foreign market provided by Latin American integration seemed difficult to achieve. Faced by these limitations, the bourgeoisies have in recent years tried to claim from imperialism a greater share of the economic surplus that each country produces – what has been called the 'wave of nationalism' in Latin America. The extent to which they have been able to do this in the different countries depends on the state of the mass movements and on the degree of North American interest in diverting investments from the traditional sectors – mainly the extractive and primary producing ones – to other sectors of the economy like the manufacturing industries, large-scale commerce and finance capital. Expressions of this 'wave of Latin American nationalism' are the C.E.C.L.A. agreements, the Bolivian pantomime, the Peruvian situation, etc.

4. Without wanting to be categorical, we have included Peru to some degree within this framework. The Peruvian generals assumed power, not on the basis of mass mobilization in that country, but of agreements made in corridors or in military barracks, with the masses remaining spectators. Even if the Peruvian masses were not on the retreat, they were at least not moving forward. Sectors of the Peruvian bourgeoisie were thereby able to open up contradictions between their interests and those of the North Americans, and also contradictions between different fractions of the bourgeoisie itself. (This analysis only tries to explain the origins of the Peruvian process and does not rule out other possibilities inherent in this process emerging from the different tendencies at present in conflict.)

5. The Chilean case is different. For at least three years, the mass mobilizations have been increasing. Allende's victory was precisely based on the aspirations of workers and peasants and was one of the expressions of that increase. The meaning of the electoral triumph goes beyond the intentions or declarations of the Popular Unity leader-

ship, for it is used by the masses to step forward in defence of their interests and to undermine the interests of the indigenous and foreign ruling classes, which are thereby threatened.

Over and above the tactical ploys and political manoeuvres of the parties which represent its interests, the Chilean bourgeoisie tries to tighten its links with imperialism and form a common front against the masses which are moving forward behind the Popular Unity. We cannot expect significant sectors of the bourgeoisie to enter an alliance with the Popular Unity in order to develop effective anti-imperialist policies. Unless, that is, the alliance with the left is based on the maintenance of the system, on increasing its profits; in other words, unless it is formed on the basis of enormous programmatic concessions by the Popular Unity.

North American Imperialism and Populist Governments in Latin America

We must also try to establish whether the world capitalist system of imperial domination can tolerate left reformist governments in Latin America.

1. The world situation since the Second World War is characterized first and foremost by the upsurge of the anti-colonial revolution throughout the world, and by imperialism's uncompromising struggle against it. The fundamental line of North American policy in the face of left-reformist governments has been explicit opposition to them. The forms and terms adopted by imperialism to deal with them have depended on the general world situation, on the North American interests involved, and on the kind of government being dealt with.

2. Since 1960, if we take the war in South East Asia as an indication, imperialism has clearly been growing more aggressive. Since 1965, leaving aside its formulations of the Alliance for Progress in relation to Latin America, imperialism, with its intervention in Santo Domingo, returned to the policy of the 'hangman' when faced with governments even of a petty-bourgeois democratic type.

3. Sometimes imperialism has, nevertheless, been obliged to accept reformist governments under conditions where it has not been able to intervene. Such cases have occurred when, for example, the balance of power has not permitted imperialism to be tied down in extensive confrontations. (At the height of the Second World War, Lázaro Cárdenas's government in Mexico nationalized petroleum without any intervention. Also populist governments like Sukharno's in Indonesia, based on an alliance between the Communist Party, sectors of the national bourgeoisie and the army, or Nkrumah's in Ghana, lasted for some time, even if both were in the end overthrown by military coups sponsored by the CIA.)

It has been a different matter when governments of that kind have appeared in the colonialist's backyard, or when imperialism has a free hand to intervene. In Guatemala in 1934, it impudently intervened against Jacobo Arbenz's government which was trying to carry through an agrarian reform damaging the interests of the United Fruit Company. The bourgeois reformist government of Goulart in Brazil which attempted timid reforms met a similar fate: it was overthrown by a military coup.

4. The present sharpness of the class struggle on an international scale is expressed by the extension of the South East Asian war to Cambodia and Laos (and probably to Thailand in the near future) and by the acuteness of the war in the Middle East. The aggressiveness of imperialism there is demonstrative of its world-wide posture. Furthermore, although it is actively involved on both these fronts, the forms that imperialism has adopted for these confrontations do not involve it directly, nor are its hands tied in such a way as to prevent intervention when threatened in its colonial backyard. The US extends the war in South East Asia on the basis of 'Vietnamization', which consists of replacing North American by native troops armed and trained by it; and in the Middle East its interests are defended by the Israeli army. The formula in both cases has the advantage of allowing the maintenance of its economy of war production. (We must be

aware that the situation in Jordan may necessitate a direct military intervention by the US in that country.)

5. In Latin America today, imperialism, with the support of the native bourgeoisies, shows a hardening of its policy. This is demonstrated by the situations in Brazil, Argentina, Uruguay and Bolivia. (In the first three, the growth of mass mobilization and the action of revolutionaries have foreclosed any possibility of 'nationalist' posturing, while in Bolivia an attempted nationalist façade failed, torn down by rising social mobilization and by the actions of the revolutionaries.)

6. In spite of the fact that the US is sometimes obliged to permit local, temporary dissent in provinces of its empire, this does not seem to be the most probable variant, at least in the long term, in Chile today. As we have already affirmed, its hard-line policy on a global and Latin-American scale does not point in that direction. That does not rule out, as a short or medium perspective, temporary toleration of a left reformist government in Chile. Moreover, it is evident that from 4 September 1970 until now the US has not shown any barefaced plans for open intervention: the necessary political atmosphere does not exist, because not all the institutional cards have yet been played. Furthermore, we cannot discard the possibility that the conflicts in South East Asia and the Middle East, and the problems of the prestige of the 'Free World's' standard-bearer – the strong internal movement against the Vietnam war, etc. – limit the US's freedom of action and extend the period of non-intervention.

But it is a different matter to confuse these conjectural limitations on the aggressiveness of imperialism with a strategic toleration of left reformism in Latin America by capitalism, thereby denying the evidence of history. Either the Popular Unity will make substantial programmatic concessions to North American capital, such that, if it expropriates investments in the extractive industries, it will open the door to investments in other sectors of the economy, thus increasing our dependence; or North American interests will be threatened and the US will turn, in the short or medium term, to a policy of intervention. This may not entail direct intervention, but could take the form of aggression by Argentina (the declaration of Admiral Isaac Rojas, the traditional representative of the Argentinian cattle-owning oligarchy, on the perils of 'communism' in Chile is suggestive); or it could take the form of supporting or igniting a confrontation between the ruling classes and workers in Chile. (Also suggestive are the accusations of the SIP, AP cables speaking of two currents – hard and soft-liners – in the USA, and the *New York Times* editorial supporting a military coup in Chile, etc.)

The Experience of Left Reformist Government

We intend to mention only a few experiences of this sort in order to stimulate militants to study them systematically and so that we can help to de-mystify the notion which is at present widespread on the Left that a left reformist government in Chile is an historical exception which has taken the Chilean Revolutionaries completely by surprise, throwing them into confusion. We will touch on a few experiences, in a very general way, always bearing in mind the enormous differences between each of them and the concrete situation we face in Chile today.

1. First of all, the revolutionary process developed by the Bolsheviks between February and October 1917 in Russia was a struggle for the seizure of power from a coalition government of the liberal bourgeoisie and the social democrats (the Mensheviks, who were Marxists) who held several ministerial posts in the central government. Throughout that period most of Lenin's and Trotsky's attacks for the Bolsheviks were justly levelled against the Mensheviks – their vacillations and half-hearted measures – in order to clarify *the differences between a left populist government and the conquest of effective power by the workers* (see *The History of the Russian Revolution* by Trotsky).

2. The German revolution of 1920 led by the Spartacists cost the lives of Karl Liebknecht and Rosa Luxemburg at the hands of the German Social Democrats, who were also Marxists and who, a few years before, had been in the same organization as Lenin and Trotsky – the Second International (see *Historia Social y Politica de Alemania* by Ramos Oliveira; the first, single volume edition, is the best).

3. In 1936 Azaña, the Popular Front Candidate, won the Presidential elections in Spain. He led a coalition consisting of bourgeois forces, the Communist Party and other parties. Soon afterwards an attempted coup by reactionary elements in the army initiated a civil war which lasted several years, cost a million deaths and, in the end, carried Franco to power. It was in the years leading up to the Second World War and the Communist Party was predominant in forming government policy. The government sought the support of Britain and France against the Rome–Berlin axis, which threatened the Soviet Union, and held back the development of the revolution, restricting its scope to the consolidation of a 'Democratic and Popular' government. The masses, not drawn into the struggle by a deepening of the revolutionary process, did not commit themselves from the start to the defence of what had been won, and only a final radicalization carried them into a desperate and heroic defence of their last strongholds. The vacillations of the anarchists (who controlled the CNT with its two million affiliated workers) and the weakness of the Revolutionary Left (represented by POUM and the left-wing of the Socialist Party) impeded the development of a revolutionary leadership for the struggle (see *La Guerra y la Revolucion de España* by Pierre Broué and Emile Temime, especially the first volume).

4. In Latin America, as we mentioned earlier, Jacobo Arbenz was elected President of Guatemala, leading a coalition which included the Communist Party. He was overthrown by Castillo Armas, encouraged and armed by the North Americans. Arbenz made the mistake of allowing

the structure of the army to remain intact, with the result that when the intervention took place and many demanded arms, weapons were not distributed to the people. He ended up in exile (see *La Batalla de Guatemala* by Guillermo Toriello).

The Chilean experience of a government of this type is well known. In the late forties, the Communist Party, in coalition with the Radical Party, elected Gabriel Videla president; soon afterwards, the Communists were outlawed, and many of them were arrested, imprisoned and sent to concentration camps (many of the Popular Unity's functionaries were ministers or officials of Gonzales Videla's government).

3

III THE ELECTORAL TRIUMPH
     OF THE POPULAR UNITY

Is the Electoral Triumph of the Popular Unity
the Definitive Victory of the Chilean Workers?

1. The Popular Unity has obtained an *electoral majority*, which has produced an impasse between the ruling classes and the workers. This electoral triumph has established the Left's theoretical right to assume power, but between that and power itself there is an enormous gulf; and in this are inserted everything from right-wing conspiracies and manoeuvres to pressures pushing the Popular Unity towards conciliation with the parties representing the interests of the ruling classes. This is the phase through which we are currently passing. The Left's electoral majority has thrown up a polarization of class forces: it has formalized on one side the workers' aspirations for political power, and on the other side the determination of the ruling classes to defend their interests; as a matter of fact both are preparing themselves for a confrontation which, sooner or later, will conclusively resolve the impasse.

2. The Popular Unity is trying to exercise power on the basis of its electoral majority. But, in the circumstances of Chile today, 'left-wing government' will simply mean that members of the Popular Unity occupy the presidency, ministerial posts, etc. As long as the apparatus of the state – its bureaucratic and military structures – remain intact, it cannot go beyond that point, since the state remains an instrument of domination and still fulfils its class function. As Lenin said, the people who really rule are the immense layer of middle functionaries, technocrats, bureaucrats and military personnel in the ministries, the under-secretariats, corporations, etc., and these people can only be displaced by a revolution.

Whether one can pass from a left-wing government through more advanced phases to the construction of socialism, depends on whether one destroys the capitalist state apparatus, on the effective participation of the masses in this process, on the revolutionary composition of the political forces leading the process, and on the measures adopted in the struggle against imperialism and in the face of finance, industrial and agrarian capital.

All the above, if it assures the revolutionary orientation of the struggle, also makes certain that the outcome will be an *armed confrontation* between the ruling classes and the workers.

3. The goal, then, is the *seizure of power by the workers*, which necessitates the destruction of the state as the bourgeoisie's instrument of domination, and the placing of the whole apparatus in the service of the workers. What we must look for is the exercise of effective power by the workers themselves, sustained on the basis of the people's possession of weapons and exercise of local power. This must take place so that all foreign capital is nationalized and all banks, rural property and factories are placed in the hands of the whole people.

To sum up, because the *Left's electoral majority* only produced an impasse between the classes in Chile, a *left-wing government*, with the state apparatus and the system of exploitation in the towns and countryside of

Chile still untouched, can only mean that the Left occupies posts in the executive; and the goal remains the struggle for the *seizure of power by the workers*, which inevitably involves an armed confrontation, sooner or later.

What is the Historical Meaning of the Left's Electoral Triumph?

1. First of all, it is necessary to establish that, electorally speaking, the Left's influence did not grow in comparison with the election of 1964 (it declined from roughly 38% to roughly 36%). The election on 4 September produced what we believed to be extremely difficult: an electoral majority for the Left. It did so for two fundamental reasons: the ruling classes were politically divided amongst themselves and faced the election with two candidates; and the election expressed the growing mobilization of the masses over the previous three years.

2. Basically, the Left's electoral majority expresses the maturity and consciousness achieved by the masses through their mobilizations in the last period. What is enormously positive about this is the evidence that large sections of the people want a socialist system, and their ability to resist estrangement at the hands of the capitalist propaganda machine operating during the election campaign.

At the level of mass consciousness, the feelings of victory and of 'the right to rule' imply an irreversible development of new forms through which the people express their aspirations to instal themselves in power. (Previously only a minority aspired to socialism, and the great mass of people could be deceived by the old Alessandrist and Frei-ist propaganda: today that is already not the case.)

The electoral triumph, regardless of whether the Popular Unity conciliates, and regardless of whether the confrontation is postponed, opens a new historical period for the masses. Great, new sections of the population have joined the struggle for socialism; and on the basis of our conviction that the ruling classes will not cede their privileges gratuitously and that a class confrontation will therefore have to take place sooner or later, the electoral triumph has assured a legitimacy and mass character to the confrontations which will precede the workers' seizure of power.

3. All that we have said convinces us that the electoral triumph constitutes an immense advance in the people's struggle for power, objectively aids the development of a revolutionary road in Chile, and therefore also benefits the Revolutionary Left.

4. The problem that revolutionaries face is the immediate and superficial view of events and the organization's practical incorporation in the process.

During the first period, the masses will confuse a left reformist government with the exercise of workers' power; they will not see a confrontation as a definite possibility – the more so while the bourgeoisie is still trying to find institutional solutions – and they will view the Popular Unity's conciliation with the Christian Democrats in a superficial way, without grasping the full gravity of its implications. For all these reasons the strategy of armed struggle which, for better or for worse, has characterized the revolutionary Left, will appear unwarranted. But to the extent that imperialism and the bourgeoisie continue to manoeuvre, the Popular Unity will be seen to be obliged to denounce the ruling classes' counter-offensive, and the distorted image of reality will dissolve, as has already begun to happen.

Moreover, in so far as our organization did not develop electoral activity, since we are not members of the Popular Unity, and because we are not linked to them in the field of practical politics, we run the risk, for a time, of appearing illegitimate and of being politically isolated. As long as the problems of defence of the electoral triumph continue to be posed, and when the possibility of a conciliation subsequently appears, this danger of isolation will also disappear. So far this has not occurred to a serious extent because of our past and present calls for the defence of the electoral triumph, and because our declarations as an organization on the popular fronts have not, up to now, enabled the reformists to attack us.

The General Characteristics of a
Possible Popular Unity Government

1. If the Popular Unity assumes office, it will do so by legal means, and it will thus be forced to govern with the capitalist state intact. It will have to govern, at least at the start of its term of office, without substantially modifying either the structure or the high and middle commands of the armed forces; it thus assures itself the permanent threat of a reactionary military coup before taking any of the measures it intends to accomplish. For the same reasons, the Popular Unity in power will be submerged by the high and middle functionaries of the previous regime, and operate within the old structures, which will certainly make its exercise of power enormously difficult. Still further, it will assume power under the prevailing legal and institutional system of capitalism, which will entangle its decisions and plans in a jungle of legalism and constitutional procedure, as bills submitted to the will of parliament, etc.

The chances of the Popular Unity substantially modifying this institutional framework, through changes in the Constitution, plebiscites, the dissolution of Parliament, etc., are limited, for they are also submerged in the same restricted legal framework.

Furthermore, these limitations, as we shall see later, are what the Christian Democrats, well aware of all this, are now trying to strengthen in their negotiations with the Popular Unity.

2. As against previous occasions, the Popular Unity obtained its electoral majority as an expression of the growing mobilization of the masses in defence of their interests. Allende found the majority that gave him victory in the more mature, more widespread and more combative aspirations of the people. Therefore, the euphoria of the triumph has already passed beyond the limits previously mentioned, thus forcing the Popular Unity, once it has assumed office, either concretely and immediately to satisfy the vehement desires of the masses, or alternatively to

confront the masses itself. From what we have said above, its ability to control the movements of the masses will be limited and possible only for a short period.

3. Thus, if the Popular Unity intends effectively to satisfy the workers' aspirations, it will be obliged to break absolutely the legal fetters upon it, radicalize its government, affirm itself in the worker and peasant movement and rapidly reach a class confrontation. If, on the other hand, it remains within the constitutional and legal framework, it will be forced to conciliate, to affirm itself with the middle strata and the bourgeois reformist parties, and, in the short or medium term, confront the mass movements, and probably see itself overthrown.

4. Furthermore, at a more concrete level, if the Popular Unity assumes office, it will inherit a difficult economic situation. The foreign debt amounts to more than two thousand million dollars and largely corresponds to loans from North American credit institutions. It will be difficult to persuade these institutions to offer the Popular Unity government the facilities they offered Frei in 1964 (when he obtained an important renegotiation of foreign debts).

The Popular Unity will have to take over a country with a low rate of economic growth, with decreased industrial, arable and cattle output, with a rate of inflation that will certainly be more than 30% this year, and with an appreciable increase in unemployment. Starting in this economic context, the Popular Unity will have difficulty resolving the workers' problems while potentially rapidly accessible sources of capital do not exist. (Nationalizations are of only limited value, unless they are massive and do not entail large-scale compensation.) Furthermore, the ruling classes are seeking every means of cutting back industrial, arable and cattle output – shortening hours of work, diminishing the sowing area, etc. – and of increasing unemployment.

Can the Popular Unity Programme be Passively Absorbed by the Capitalist System?

1. The starting points for this analysis are the official versions of the programme and Salvador Allende's declarations during and after the campaign. We will not take into account some recent signs of imminent dilution in the programme (Cademartori's verbal insistence on three banks, Labarca's distinction between Yarur the 'bad entrepreneur' and Hirmas the 'good entrepreneur', distinctions made by radicals between 'big monopolies' and 'small monopolies', Millas' agreement with the management of MADECO, etc.).

A study of the possibilities of the ruling class accepting the Popular Unity's programme cannot be based on an abstract assessment of the viability of the theoretical economic model formulated in that programme. Indeed, seen only from this angle, it *is* practicable and similar economic plans have been carried out in concrete historical situations – for example, during the NEP period in the twenties in the USSR, in the fifties in China, etc. But, in those countries the model was imposed on the ruling classes after an authentic revolutionary process. We must start from the actual situation in Chile, which demonstrates that its implementation must damage powerful vested interests which would have difficulty passively accepting it. We must also be clear that the fundamental problems do not arise simply over the viability of such and such an economic measure, or over the extent of the capital affected by these possible measures; they stem basically from the national and international decisions and political consequences implied by each economic measure (property rights, the possible example to the rest of Latin America of the feasibility of expropriating North American enterprises without compensation, and the possible creation of blocs like Havana–Lima–Santiago in opposition to the 'great powers' of Latin America like Brazil and Argentina, etc.).

Here we will consider our own programme, and that of

the Popular Unity in general terms only, leaving a deeper analysis of this theme for a special survey now being made.

2. The points in our programme (August 1965) are based on the need to destroy the capitalist state. Our programme, is not simply anti-imperialist and anti-monopoly, but is anti-capitalist and anti-monopoly; in other words, while we also in the first phase seek to protect the small agricultural proprietor, the small merchant and the small industrialist, we do not believe that there are sectors of the industrial agrarian bourgeoisie with which we can form alliances; still less do we seek to protect such sectors. (We do not recognize the existence of that 'middle bourgeoisie' under cover of which the Popular Unity in a confused way makes concessions to the ruling classes.)

We believe that the Chilean ruling class embraces the North American ruling classes and the industrial, financial and agrarian bourgeoisie. We do not recognize the existence of 'good' or 'bad' industrial or agrarian entrepreneurs. Moreover, for us what is involved is not simply the enlargement of the state sphere of the economy while significant sectors of big capitalist agricultural industry are allowed to survive and develop; further, we do not recognize the existence of an agrarian feudalism which has to be fought. To sum up, we put forward a programme which is anti-imperialist and anti-capitalist – a fundamentally socialist programme; we do not subscribe to the positions of some of the predominant forces inside the Popular Unity, such as the Communist Party, who say: the programme must be anti-imperialist, yes, but also anti-monopoly, anti-feudal, and democratic.

3. In spite of this, we believe that the Popular Unity's programme as it stands does attack some vital nuclei of capitalism, such as the foreign enterprises, financial capital, the monopoly sector of big industry, and latifundism. Thus, if this programme is implemented, it will provoke a counter-offensive from the imperialists and the bourgeoisie; this, combined with the freeing of the masses' energies and aspirations, will rapidly force a radicalization of the process. Therefore, while the Popular Unity's pro-

gramme is not the same as ours, we will support and push forward the realization of these fundamental measures.

4. We affirm that if the Popular Unity's programme is carried out, it will attack vital nuclei of capitalism and therefore the present capitalist, dependent system will not be able passively to aborb it.

Regarding its policy on agrarian matters, we believe that sectors of the industrial bourgeoisie may support measures which stimulate greater industrialization of agriculture and cattle production, in order to increase production in this sector: this will lower the cost of living and will therefore permit reductions in the cost of industrial wages; on the other hand it will raise the standard of living of the rural population, thus drawing nearly three million into the consumer market for industrial production, whose development has been blocked by the lack of an internal market. But at the same time the bourgeoisie cannot accept expropriation of most of the agricultural enterprises, unless it is accompanied by excellent compensation, since agricultural entrepreneurs are at present largely identical with, or belong to the same families as, the industrial entrepreneurs and bank owners.

The Popular Unity has emphasized its intention of nationalizing copper and all the great mining concerns. It is well known that, following the recent rise in demand for copper and its high price on the world market, enormous sources of copper production were opened up in other parts of the world, and in addition the long-term substitution of other metals for copper is assured. North American capital in Latin America has, moreover, tended to shift from traditional sectors of investment (in Chile fundamentally mining) to manufacturing industry, finance and commerce, thus greatly diminishing the relative importance of North American investments in the great Chilean mines. Thus, although North American investors have no wish to lose the short term benefits that copper has brought with its continued high prices over the last period, we cannot rule out the possibility that they, and therefore the State Department, might accept this specific kind of 'nationalization', provided they were assured satisfactory compensation on reasonable terms and the opportunity to shift investments to other areas of the economy like manufacturing industry. (This explains their complacent acceptance of the Frei government's 'negotiated nationalization'.) The other great mining concerns are not in exactly the same position, but their relative importance is not so great.

It is a different matter in the case of the so-called monopoly industry which the Popular Unity has promised to nationalize. The fundamental interests of the most dynamic and important sector of the Chilean bourgeoisie lie in this sector of the economy. Furthermore, since North American investment is being directed towards this sector, the trend that has been observed in Chile and throughout Latin America is for the bourgeoisie to continue its growth starting from an alliance with North American capital in this sector and directing itself to a search for foreign outlets through the formation of Latin-American common markets. Passive acceptance of nationalization in this sector of the economy, either by the native or foreign ruling classes, whatever the form or amount of compensation, would mean economic and historical suicide for the bourgeoisie and the system of imperialist domination – and this is out of the question without bloodshed.

The Chilean banks, representing the highest point of capitalist development, also belong to the most important sectors of the bourgeoisie and imperialism. The bourgeoisie will not freely abandon the economic function of distributing credit at its convenience: and the benefits it obtains from the administration of credit are extensive. Although rational administration of credit by the state can benefit small merchants, farmers and industrialists, the nationalization of banking involves depriving the bourgeoisie of one of its important functions and damaging powerful interests. We do not believe it possible to carry out a measure of that nature with the passive acceptance of those who would be witnessing the destruction of the bases of their wealth and power.

5. For all these reasons, we consider that if the Popular Unity tries to carry through its programme, it will be thrown into a class confrontation, either before or during the period in which it attempts to implement the measures analysed above. Whatever form this takes it will certainly be violent. Clearly, events will proceed in a different way if the Popular Unity restricts itself to measures of the following kind: expropriation of some agrarian property as a means of stimulating the industrialization of agriculture and the rural population's incorporation into the national consumption market; the nationalization of copper, offering substantial compensation; tolerance of the diversion of North American investments to manufacturing industry; full nationalization of only some of the banks and big industries, allowing and protecting the growth of others and the displacement of quantities of capital from the former to the latter. This would amount to compromising its political programme, maintaining the system of imperialist domination and developing more advanced forms of the capitalist system! This would allow the Popular Unity, if the ruling classes do not overthrow it before, to use its initial public image and the immediate effect of its programme to maintain its appearance of being a 'popular government' for a short period; but in the short or medium term it would be forced to confront the masses whose aspirations will not have been satisfied.

(*Publisher's Note:* Sections iv and v which follow in the original contain a more detailed analysis of the above and have been omitted in this edition.)

VI GENERAL CONCLUSIONS ON THE PRESENT POLITICAL SITUATION

Before formulating our policy and posing our tasks in relation to the present political situation, we want to sum up our analysis of the political situation in the country after the September elections, to facilitate the understanding of this document.

1. Through the intensification of the class struggle in Chile, conditions no longer exist for the long-term survival of populist governments which can ally with important sections of the bourgeoisie, thereby developing anti-imperialist policies. Instead the bourgeoisie will seek a common front with imperialism against the mass movement.

2. At present imperialism has a hard attitude towards left reformist governments in Latin America and throughout the world and it does not feel that its hands are tied or that it is restrained from intervening. In the short or medium term, unless the Popular Unity makes important concessions, it will adopt a policy of intervention in Chile – this can take various forms.

3. This is not the first time in the world that revolutionaries have found themselves confronted by a left reformist government. Historical experience demonstrates that if these governments do not radicalize themselves and opt for class confrontations, they always end up by being overthrown in the clamour of the class struggle. To our knowledge, past experience confirms the sentence of the old French revolutionary, Saint-Just: 'Whoever makes a revolution by half, only succeeds in digging his own grave.'

4. The Popular Unity's electoral victory establishes merely the theoretical right of the Left to assume office. If it does become the government while the capitalist state apparatus and the class structure remain intact, this will mean nothing more than the Left's spokesmen taking up ministerial posts. The goal is the conquest of power by the workers and that involves without doubt a class confrontation, since it damages class interests.

5. The Left's electoral triumph constitutes an enormous advance for the workers' struggles, draws new sectors of the masses into the struggle for socialism, and assures the legitimacy and mass character of the future social confrontation. It therefore favours the development of the revolution and for that reason is also beneficial for the revolutionary left. The apparent difficulty lies in the fact that the armed struggle seems unnecessary and the revo-

lutionaries seem in danger of being isolated through failing to develop electoral activity.

6. In assuming office, the Popular Unity will do so with the capitalist state apparatus intact, thus assuring the permanency of the traditional armed forces, the bureaucratic apparatus and the legal system; this in turn assures the permanent risk of a reactionary military coup, difficulty in operating as a government, and the possibility of being entangled in a jungle of legalisms, which is just what the Christian Democrats are trying to ensure. At the same time, the Popular Unity owed its victory to the fact that the aspirations of the masses had become broader and more mature, and the masses will seek to satisfy them; this will force the Popular Unity into the following dilemma: either class conciliation followed by a confrontation with the masses; or radicalization and confrontation with the ruling classes.

7. Although the Popular Unity's programme is not identical with ours, it proposes to attack vital nuclei of the capitalist system and damage powerful interests; if it is implemented, it will unleash an imperialist and bourgeois counter-offensive, which, combined with the liberation of energies at the level of the masses, will radicalize the process; for this reason we will push for the implementation of the measures proposed in the Popular Unity's programme.

8. Our strategy of the conquest of power through the armed struggle is more valid today than ever, since the confrontation has only been postponed. The final form of the struggle for the conquest of power will be irregular, protracted war, whatever may be the different forms it assumes at the start, just after the electoral triumph. The methods of direct action, direct mass mobilization, and participation in popular street mobilizations are still clearly valid and their content, form and timing will have to be adapted to the political situation of the moment.

9. Our electoral policy was in essence correct, though we underestimated the Popular Unity's possibilities for manoeuvre and the political-tactical weakness that the ruling

class could possess in the event of the Left's electoral triumph. For this reason we concentrated on working out policies for the eventuality of the Popular Unity's electoral defeat or for an immediate attack in the event of its triumph. In spite of this our policy gave us political legitimacy in the eyes of the *Allendista* masses and gave us a good basis for working out a policy for the defence of the victory, for pressing for the implementation of the programme, and for the struggle against class conciliation.

10. After its electoral defeat the ruling classes retreated politically. Leaderless, lacking political banners with even a semblance of legitimacy, in an unpropitious political atmosphere, with the Christian Democrats also defeated, and with a momentary loss of monolithism in the armed forces, they could not openly and effectively oppose the Popular Unity's assumption of office.

11. The heterogeneous political and social composition of the Popular Unity and the lack of military force at its disposal, impeded its path towards government. By basing its right to rule only on the legitimacy of its electoral majority and on the support of an organized mass which was not actively mobilized, the Popular Unity allowed itself two possible roads to government: either acceptance of negotiations and pressure, class conciliation and the shackling of the future government; or effective mass mobilizations, on the basis of which it would demonstrate its right to rule and impose its own terms.

12. It is clear to us that from 4 September onwards a power vacuum has existed in Chile; neither the government, nor the Christian Democrats, nor the armed forces, nor the Popular Unity have the initiative or control the situation.

13. The momentary setback for the ruling classes must not be confused with their strategic defeat. They still hold intact the state apparatus, the military apparatus, the bureaucratic machine, economic power and legality and the resolute support of imperialism. With this they intend unscrupulously to defend their power and wealth.

14. In actual fact the ruling classes try various strate-

gies, from the conspiracies of the extreme right, to playing their last legal cards such as re-election at the Congress
Plenum. In spite of this we believe their predominant
strategy will be to allow Allende to assume office in order
to entangle him in the legalistic jungle under permanent
threat of a military coup; they will thereby hope to obstruct the carrying out of his plans and the satisfaction of
the masses' aspirations; they intend to promote the decline
of industrial, agricultural and cattle output, the rise of inflation and unemployment, and then, in order to 'save the
country from chaos', when Allende has already lost his
prestige among the masses, they will overthrow him. All
this would give the bourgeoisie and imperialism the advantage of historically discrediting the Left's road for
Latin America.

15. We cannot rule out a confrontation prior to 4
November or a radicalization of the Popular Unity government in the face of a reactionary counter-offensive which
forces it to base itself on the mass movement to carry it
into a class confrontation of historic significance.

VII   OUR POLICY

To formulate a policy for a situation like the present, one
which is uncertain and ill-defined, does not involve trying
to play the role of a sorcerer or soothsayer in politics.
Many fundamental questions are still unanswerable, others
allow us to outline possibilities and a few are already
answered by the facts. The Popular Unity is not yet in
office and as yet we do not know what the exact composition of its government will be; we do not have a
concrete idea of what its first measures will be, and on a
more immediate level no one as yet knows what answer it
will give to the Christian Democrats.

As events develop they will define the questions and
only then will more clear and categorical policies emerge
as necessary and possible. We are concerned here to ap-
praise reality in general terms, assessing the factors in
play and the predominant forces; on this basis we can

understand the process, the factors determining the possible directions that events could follow. Further, we will try below to define the most likely tendencies, so that we can back those aspects which coincide with our policy and combat those which oppose us.

Policy of Accepting and Defending the Electoral Triumph

1. We consider most urgent, as a way of establishing our legitimacy among the *Allendista* masses, for us, as an organization and in the mass fronts, to recognize Allende as president; we have already done this to some extent through declarations that for us 'the people have already elected the President'. As we do so we must clearly establish that in doing this we are reaffirming our programme; that is to say, it means the workers have conquered the right to appropriate for themselves Chilean and foreign enterprises, factories, banks and estates.

2. We must formulate calls for the defence of the Left's electoral triumph against right-wing manoeuvres; we must expose the dangers and the intentions of the Right to block Allende's assumption of office and implementation of the programme; we must argue that the only way to defend Allende and ensure the passing of the programme is through mass mobilizations starting from the fronts, the elaboration of a strategy and its technical and military preparation.

3. We must always make clear that our attitude is not opportunistic, that we do not develop electoral activity, that we push forward mobilization of the masses for their own interests and that we work for the defence of the triumph. We must always explain the difference between an electoral majority, a leftist government and the conquest of power by the workers.

4. We must take up the political slogans put forward by Allende (not recognized by the Communist Party): 'A factory which sabotages production is a factory which will be occupied by the workers'; 'Occupy estates and factories if the triumph of the Left is not accepted', etc.

5. In so far as the 'power vacuum' is prolonged, we

will try to become 'the best sword' against the diehard reactionaries in the eyes of the masses. We must try to take the initiative in the struggle against the diehards, through mobilizations of the Mass Fronts or in the streets, or even through actions, which will necessarily have to be 'sympathetic' and 'clear', in that they must not contribute to creating 'chaos' and 'provocation' in the eyes of the workers.

The Struggle Against Conciliation

1. We shall have to strive to prevent a conciliation of the Popular Unity government with the Christian Democrats, for it is in the latter that the objective elements trying to put a brake on the process are to be found. For this purpose we must strike at the Christian Democrats, recall Frei's policy of giving in on the copper mines, the El Salvador and Port Montt massacres, the tortures and political prisoners, and his repressive, anti-popular attitude towards mobilizations of the workers, peasants, squatters and students.

2. We must state publicly that the Christian Democracy was repudiated by the people in September, that the people have already elected their president, that there is nothing to negotiate, that Senators and Deputies have nothing to do. In our relationships with other political organizations and the mass fronts we must advance the idea of a struggle against conciliation, without attacking the Popular Unity Government and all the while defending its programme.

A Policy of Radicalizing and Deepening the Process

1. We must activate mass commitment to the defence of the victory through demands for measures corresponding to popular and general aspirations, such as a basic wage of one thousand pesos, a single standard family allowance equal to the highest one operating at present, the freezing of prices as from 1 January.

2. We will press in the Mass Fronts for the raising of demands such as the non-payment of *corvée* quotas, the

right to a field and a house, the right to land, a fair wage and workers' control of production, banks and foreign enterprises, the nationalization of private education, free entrance to the universities, the right to vote for the armed forces, etc. In accordance with the political situation, we will progressively drive forward mobilizations behind these demands.

3. We shall strive to implant this process of defence in the poorest layers of society, as a way of ensuring that the process takes a revolutionary and socialist course. Through meetings and concentration on the corresponding mass fronts, through the raising of demands and the subsequent mobilization, through leaflets, and manifestos, through wall slogans and posters, etc. we will call for the organization of Committees for the Defence of Victory, where we will seek to organize workers, peasants, squatters and students on clear political lines, together with the rest of the revolutionary Left and with those revolutionary groups which exist in the ranks of the traditional Left; thereby we will strike at the Right, attack the Christian Democrats, push for a strategy for the defence of the victory on a mass level, etc.

4. We will formulate a policy for the armed forces, especially directed towards the junior officers, the NCOs and the troops; we will centre our demands around salaries, bonuses, social security, housing, relations with high officialdom, the right to vote, etc. We will develop our work of recruitment and penetration of all branches throughout the country.

5. We will declare that the defence of the triumph lies on the level of mass mobilization more than on possible institutional supports. We shall try to displace the centre of decision-making from the Moneda* and the corridors of Congress to the mobilized mass fronts. We will raise slogans such as: 'Allende to the Moneda, Power to the People', 'All Power to the Workers', 'The people have already chosen, *merde* to Parliament', etc.

* The Presidential Palace.

Necessary developments of our policy

1. If indeed we acknowledge the Popular Unity government, if we work for its defence and press for the realization of its programme, we will nevertheless not officially and formally join the government whilst questions relating to the composition of the government forces, and its concrete political line etc, remain confused. In so far as it radicalizes the process, mobilizes the masses and confronts the reactionary counter-offensive, we will modify our political attitude. In so far as it conciliates the Christian Democrats over fundamental issues, allows itself to be shipwrecked and does not carry out its programme, we will maintain our political independence, supporting positive measures and fighting regressive ones, as well as demanding that whatever it did not carry out be completed.

2. Although we shall be working in the Popular Unity committees, which by their composition and activity are going in a positive direction, we will not officially join the Popular Unity whilst the specific administrative and political weight of forces such as the Radical Party in the government remain unknown. We will call for the formation of Committees for the Defence of the Electoral Triumph through mass fronts in which the workers and the revolutionaries will work together.

3. We will seek to develop our relations with the revolutionary organizations and the revolutionary sectors that exist in the traditional Left. We shall maintain our relations with the Socialist Party.

4. We shall maintain our clandestine, compartmentalized, politico-military structure for as long as the capitalist system exists and power has not been conquered by the workers. Moreover we will try to develop our operational apparatus for as long as there is a possibility of a confrontation, and organize forms which will allow for the success of our strategies of street struggle or the struggles of big mass contingents.

5. For these same reasons, these operations will continue to be forms of struggle which we ourselves can em-

ploy. We will be able to adapt their scope, content and timing in order not to provide fodder for the bourgeoisie and imperialism, while looking after the survival, development, and political presence of the organization. In the short term these actions will probably consist initially of operations against the plots of the extreme Right.

6. If the Popular Unity grants pardons to political prisoners, this will have to be accepted, in as much as these people are only guilty of struggling against the system of social robbery, and are innocent in the eyes of the workers. If moreover, on its own initiative, the Popular Unity grants an amnesty to those who remain persecuted today, we shall accept it also. The condition of 'illegality' does not stem from the will of revolutionaries, for it is governments which establish persecution. Clandestinity and security measures for as long as the armed apparatus of the state is not effectively in the service of the workers, the workers have not seized power, and the possibility of a confrontation exists, is quite another question. Clandestinity will continue to be necessary in varying degree and will be operated without unnecessary exaggeration, and in conformity with the concrete circumstances of reality.

7. In the mass fronts we will adopt a policy of recognition and defence of the electoral triumph, of raising platforms of demands, and supporting mass mobilizations arising from these fronts. In all probability, we will only call for mass mobilizations around far-reaching demands at conjunctures of confrontation, or after 4 November, according to the course taken by events.